Daniel Francis

A Road for Canada

The Illustrated Story of the Trans-Canada Highway

Stanton Atkins & Dosil Publishers

CONTENTS

The Trans-Canada Highway winds across the red soil of Prince Edward Island.

The Trans-Canada Highway west of Field with the President Range in the background.

The Road is Open

"This highway, may it serve to bring Canadians closer together, may it bring to all Canadians a renewed determination to individually do their part to make this nation greater and greater still, worthy of the destiny that the Fathers of Confederation had expected when through their act of faith they made it possible. Above all, I express the hope and the prayer today that this highway will always serve the cause of peace, that it will never hear the marching tramp of warlike feet."

Prime Minister John Diefenbaker, 3 September 1962, at official opening of the Trans-Canada Highway

AT 3:05 on the afternoon of September 3, 1962, under a clear blue sky and surrounded by the glistening peaks of the Selkirk mountain range, Prime Minister John Diefenbaker, wearing a hard hat he had borrowed for the occasion, tamped down the final square of asphalt in the Rogers Pass roadbed and declared the Trans-Canada Highway officially open.

It was typical of the day that at that precise moment the sound system failed, and Diefenbaker's words were lost to the onlookers who had assembled to watch the historic occasion. The ceremony had not gone according to plan. As the *Globe and Mail* reported, most of the fourteen dignitaries who were scheduled to speak ignored their time limits, and the speeches dragged on for more than two hours under the blazing sun. One of the worst offenders was the federal minister of public works, British Columbia's own E. Davie Fulton, who insisted on itemizing how much money the federal government had spent on highway construction in each of the provinces and territories. When it came his turn, the representative from Saskatchewan, whether distracted by the glorious view, addled by the heat, or bored by the length of the speeches, declared how impressed he was at being in Quebec. British Columbia's minister of highways, Phil Gaglardi, who was a preacher when he wasn't being a politician, declared,

1

"I want to thank God personally for the beautiful weather He has given us." The customary singing of *O Canada* had not taken place because the bus carrying the instruments belonging to the band of the Princess Patricia's Canadian Light Infantry had taken a wrong turn on the way up the highway from Calgary. The bus arrived in time for the band to end the festivities with *God Save the Queen*, however, and the crowd of close to 3,000 people sang lustily, thankful that the interminable ceremony appeared to be over and they would soon be able to get into the shade and eat some lunch.

In his own speech, Prime Minister Diefenbaker had observed that the Trans-Canada Highway had brought "a renewed sense of national unity" to the country, a remark which must have raised the eyebrows of his assembled colleagues. For while the highway project was many things, a force for national unity was not one of them, at least not yet. For years, Quebec had not signed on to the project, claiming it was an intrusion into the province's area of constitutional responsibility. Newfoundland and New Brunswick both boycotted the opening ceremony, New Brunswick because in the whole province there was apparently no one available to attend and Newfoundland because it was still unhappy with the cost-sharing agreement. Another conspicuous absentee was the host premier, British Columbia's own W.A.C. Bennett. "Wacky", as he was fondly known to provincial voters, had built his career on Ottawa-bashing and he was not about to show up at a federal ceremony on his home turf. Especially since he had already opened the highway at an official ceremony of his own a month earlier, on July 30. On that occasion, Bennett had snipped a ribbon near Revelstoke and christened the new road "BC Highway No. 1", no mention of Canada at all. "There was one of the most peculiar, self-centred actions that I've ever known," Diefenbaker later recalled. But to Bennett, it was all part of jockeying for political advantage.

Opposite: Baking under a hot sun, the impatient on-lookers who have come to Rogers Pass to witness the highway's opening wait for the politicians to finish their speeches. The highway "has generated a renewed sense of national unity," Prime Minister Diefenbaker told them. "It has brought about a sense of oneness from the Atlantic to the Pacific Ocean, comparable to that which moved Canadians when the first Canadian transcontinental railway was completed."

This historic plaque at Chippewa Falls, Ontario, mounted on a cairn 55 kilometres north of Sault Ste. Marie, where the road skirts scenic Batchawana Bay, marks the highway's halfway point between St. John's, Newfoundland, and Victoria, British Columbia.

Why should federal politicians get any credit, he argued, when they weren't contributing to the other highways in the province, nor were they contributing to maintaining the Trans-Canada?

Whichever ceremony is accepted as the "official" one, the opening of the 147-kilometre section of road through Rogers Pass marked the completion of the first continuous, all-season, two-lane road across Canada. To prove it, an inaugural motorcade of eleven cars (one representing the federal government and one for each province) had driven the route that summer, all the way from St. John's in Newfoundland to Victoria on the Pacific Ocean. True, parts of the highway still

were not paved, and wouldn't be for another three years. But that needn't discourage any intrepid motorist who wanted to see the country. A project first envisioned by B.C.'s Governor James Douglas 103 years earlier was finally a reality.

As Prime Minister Diefenbaker remarked, it was fitting that one of the mountain peaks overlooking the opening ceremony was named for John A. Macdonald. After all, it was Macdonald who had been such a fierce proponent of the transcontinental railway, the first "road" across the country. Completed in 1885, the Canadian Pacific Railway was hailed as a great achievement in nation-building. More than just an iron road, it was con-

sidered to have provided the transportation link that made the country itself possible. Doubtless Diefenbaker, whose government had just suffered a humiliating rebuff at the polls that had reduced it to a minority position, hoped that by championing the highway as Canada's second "National Dream" and by transforming it into a symbol of national unity he might burnish his own place in Canadian history.

There were important details Diefenbaker found it convenient not to mention in his speech. Such as the fact that construction was years behind schedule and hundreds of millions of dollars over budget. Or that, technically, the road was not finished at all. He and the other

dignitaries preferred to emphasize what a tremendous achievement the highway was. And it was. At 7,714 kilometres, the Trans-Canada Highway crosses six time zones and remains the world's longest continuous trans-national highway. Or, as journalist Walter Stewart preferred, it is the world's only national roadway with "two beginnings and no end. You start from mile zero on Water Street in downtown St. John's, Newfoundland," Stewart wrote, "drive 7,714 kilometres and finish up in Beacon Hill in downtown Victoria, where the sign reads – guess what? – Mile 0."

The highway passes through steep river canyons so deep that the sunlight only penetrates for a few minutes in the day, across boggy swamps that freeze in winter and become quagmires after the thaw, around lakes, through virgin forest, and over the broken lunar landscape of the Canadian Shield. Out west, builders literally moved mountains to complete the project. One enterprising journalist calculated that if all the earth and rock used to build the highway were dumped into railway freight cars the resulting train would be long enough to circle the earth five times at the equator. The road had to be hard-surfaced with asphalt for its entire route, and built to the very latest safety and design standards. In every way, the Trans-Canada Highway rivalled the transcontinental railway as a great national achievement. Where did this ambitious, high-priced, geography-defying project originate? And did it succeed in becoming a symbol of Canadian unity?

Three models pose beside the mile zero sign in Beacon Hill Park, Victoria, B.C. It's not surprising that the maple leaf emblem was adopted for the distinctive Trans-Canada Highway 1 sign. By the 1960s the maple leaf, which had symbolized the country since colonial times, said Canada more clearly than any other emblem. It appeared on the earliest coins and postage stamps. "The Maple Leaf Forever," written by Alexander Muir in 1867, was the nation's patriotic song. The maple leaf adorned the overseas headstones of Canadian soldiers who died in the First World War and was used widely on military badges and medals.

Athletes wore the insignia during international competitions. Three years after the Trans-Canada opened, the maple leaf would become the dominant element in the new national flag. In the words of Prime Minister Lester Pearson, the maple leaf was "Canada's own and only Canada's."

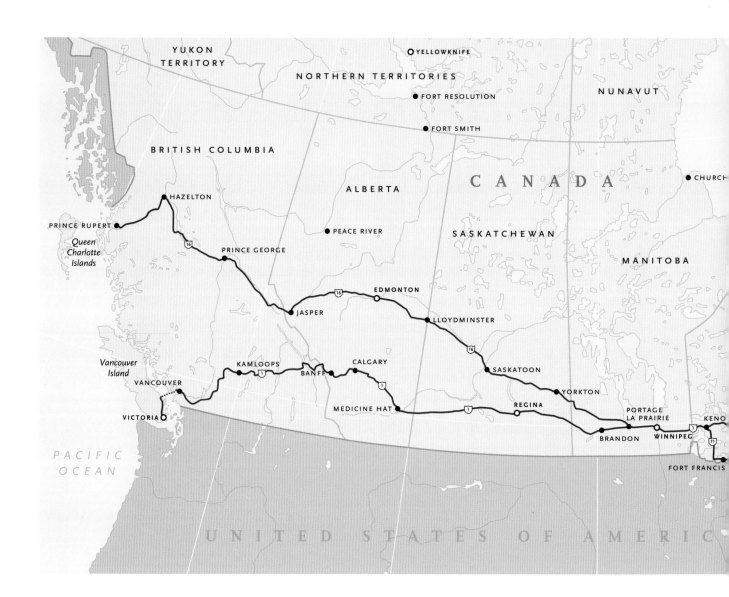

As this map shows, the Trans-Canada is not a single highway. The country is too complicated for that. Originally conceived by planners as the shortest practicable east-west route, the main highway veers off in different directions as it makes its way from sea to sea. Rather than a Trans-Canada Highway, modern planners now talk about a National Highway System, a network of main roads totalling tens of thousands of kilometres that link the country's major communities to each other and to the United States.

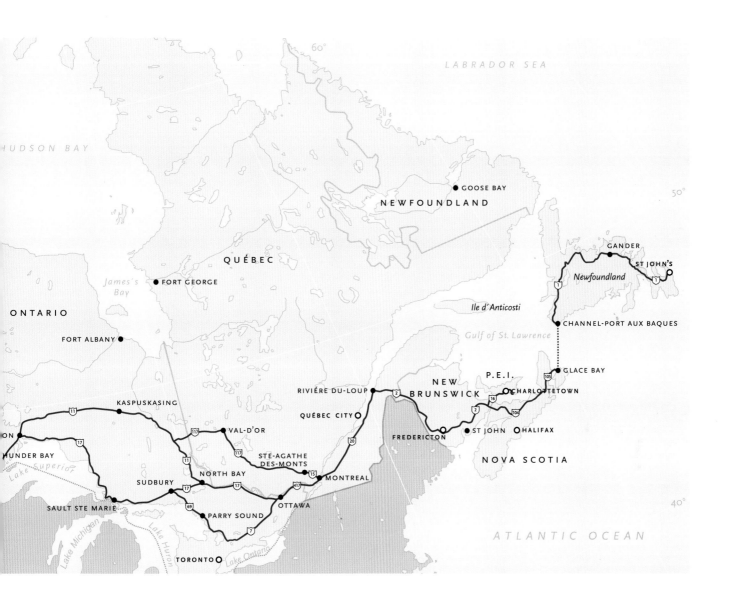

Cap d'Or in the Bay of Fundy,
a short drive off the
Trans-Canada in Nova Scotia.

The Race for Gold

CHAPTER ONE

"Outside a railway carriage there is no hope for comfortable travel in present-day Canada."
Maclean's, 1912

IT IS IMPOSSIBLE to say that construction of the Trans-Canada Highway began on a specific date because the project incorporated a variety of already existing roadways, some of them going back many years. It is possible to say that organized lobbying for a national road began on an early May day in 1912 when a group of automobile enthusiasts gathered outside the town of Alberni on the far west coast of Vancouver Island. The event was sponsored by the Canadian Highway Association, a group which had been formed in New Westminster the previous year to work for the completion of a trans-continental highway. At Alberni, they were joined by members of the Victoria Automobile Club who had driven up from the capital in a 50-car convoy across the newly-opened Malahat Highway. The purpose of the gathering was to publicize the project by unveiling the first signpost. The sign read "Canadian Highway" and marked mile zero on a road that had yet to be built. (Shortly after the sign was erected, it was stolen one night and repositioned inside the city limits of Port Alberni, Alberni's

rival community. The original promoters stole it back and chained a fierce-looking bull terrier to the post to make sure the theft did not happen again.)

Looking back, one cannot help but admire the audacity of this small band of automaniacs standing in the rain outside Alberni. The age of the automobile had hardly begun and here they were proposing that a highway be built from sea to distant sea and that it be completed in just four years. At the time there were fewer than 50,000 licensed automobiles in the whole country. British Columbia had just 4,000; Nova Scotia a mere 911. These were not large enough numbers to convince public officials of the need for local roads, let alone a national highway. In Prince Edward Island, antagonism from farmers against the horseless carriage was so strong that the legislature had voted to ban them, and the island remained car-free until 1913, at which point motorized vehicles were allowed on the road for three days of the week. The speed limit on provincial highways across the country was 30 kilometres an hour, and

11

Motoring enthusiasts gather at Alberni, British Columbia, on May 4, 1912, to kick off the campaign for a Canadian Highway. B.C.'s lieutenant governor, T.W. Paterson, was in attendance, along with local politicians from Vancouver, Victoria, Nanaimo and Alberni. The event was sponsored by the Canadian Highway Association, which predicted that in five years a modern road would stretch across the continent. The prediction was off by forty-five years. Note the variety of coats, caps and hats worn by motorists to ward off the weather. Automobiles still went topless, leaving drivers exposed to the elements.

Licence plates evolved along with vehicles. In 1903 Ontario was the first province to require vehicles to be licensed. (The same law set a sixteen-kilometre-an-hour speed limit for city streets.) Two years later Ontario motorists were required to paint the licence number on their vehicle. In other provinces it was up to owners to fashion a licence plate out of whatever material was at hand. The story goes that an Alberta motorist, having been issued licence number 1, simply attached an upright broomstick to his vehicle. The next step was goverment-issued licence plates, introduced in most provinces by the First World War.

Top: A 1912 plate from British Columbia with numbers riveted to a leather pad in a metal frame.

Bottom: A homemade 1907 leather plate that hung from the vehicle by a strap.

frightening the horses still earned motorists a heavy fine. The roads that were being built led south toward the American border, not east-west through the vast expanses of the Canadian interior. The only concrete highway in the country was a 16-kilometre stretch outside Montreal.

The Canadian Highway Association was undaunted by such challenges. Members were determined to rally public opinion behind the highway project. As a publicity stunt they offered a gold medal to the first motorist driving an all-Canadian route from Halifax to the Pacific. (A pair of American motorists, Dr. A. Nelson Jackson and his chauffeur, Sewall Crocker, were the first to drive across the United States, from San Francisco to New York, in 1903, and their feat had been duplicated many times by 1912.) The medal was donated by A.E. Todd, a Victoria salmon canner, president of the Victoria Automobile Club and proud owner of a shiny new Cadillac. The medal was intended to encourage some adventurous motorist to attempt a continental crossing, and in the process stir up public interest in better roads.

And so begins the saga of Thomas Wilby and Jack Haney.

THOMAS WILBY was a British journalist, formerly a foreign correspondent, who had settled with his wife in New York where he began leading motor tours and writing about them. In 1912, he decided that it would make a good story if he were able to drive the "all-Red" route from Atlantic to Pacific; that is, a route totally within Canada (which, like every other member of the British Empire, was coloured red on maps). He approached different car companies with his idea, and the Reo Motor Car Company agreed to supply him with a car and driver, a 23-year-old mechanic from Indiana named Jack Haney. Haney began working for Reo in Lansing, Michigan, in 1905, about the same time as pioneer manufacturer Ransom E. Olds established the company. A few years later Olds opened a Canadian subsidiary in St. Catharines, Ontario, and Haney moved north to become the branch plant's chief mechanic. He was the obvious person to accompany Wilby on his cross-country adventure.

Employees of the Reo Motor Car Company of Canada gather at their St. Catharines, Ontario, factory for an outing – complete with brass band, judging by the instruments held by some of the excursionists. The Canadian factory, a branch plant of the America company, opened in 1909.

At right is the logo for the American company, based in Lansing, Michigan. Reo Canada used a similar insignia with the wings turned downward. The Reo got its name from the initials of the company's founder, Ransom Eli Olds.

The Reo Special Touring Car was a high, handsome vehicle, state-of-the-art for its time, with wooden spoke wheels and a 30-horsepower, four-cylinder engine. But it had its inconveniences. It had to be cranked to start, and when darkness approached the driver had to stop to light the acetylene headlamps by hand. There were no side windows to keep out the elements, and one foot pedal was both clutch and brake. In those days garages were few and far between so motorists carried their own tool kit. Haney had fitted out two trunks with reserve gas tanks, tins of oil, spare inner tubes and a pump, chains for the wheels, hooks for hauling out of the mud, and a block and tackle that would turn out to be more useful than he could have anticipated.

Wilby and Haney were a mismatched pair and soon grew to loathe each other. The 45-year-old Englishman was a pompous snob with an eye for the limelight. When he arrived in Halifax to begin the trip, his baggage amounted to a single change of socks, serving notice that he expected to be waited on by his driver, whom he asked to address him as "Sir". In the book Wilby published about the trip, *A Motor Tour Through Canada*, he did not once mention the younger man by name. Always he was "the chauffeur". Nor did Wilby feel any obligation to help his driver when the Reo bogged down in the mud or pitched over into a ditch, preferring to scribble in his notebook while his partner did the heavy lifting. Not long into the trip, Haney was confiding to his diary, "I am heartily sick of my companion and will be mightily glad when the trip is over. He is too damn selfish." But like it or not, the two were stuck with each other for the duration.

Canada in 1912 was a country enjoying an unprecedented era of prosperity and growth. The population in the previous decade had jumped by more than a third to about 7.2 million people and was still growing. These new Canadians came mostly from the United States and Europe, including, for the first time, sizeable numbers of Germans, Scandinavians, Ukrainians and Slavic peoples. In other words, not only was the country larger, it

This is the 1912 Reo Special Touring Car manufactured at the St. Catharines plant and used by Thomas Wilby and Jack Haney to cross the country. One of these vehicles cost about $1,500. Reo Canada stayed in business until 1915, when the factory was turned over to war production. The company revived in 1931 in a former Dodge plant in Toronto, but by 1936 it had ceased producing cars and began focusing on trucks instead. Its most famous product was the Reo Speed-wagon, a forerunner of the pickup truck.

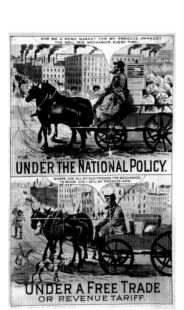

was also much more ethnically diverse. The economy was firing on all cylinders, fuelled by foreign investment and exports of wheat, forest products and minerals. Canadians remained in the grip of a railway-building mania as the Canadian Pacific was joined by two other transcontinental lines. In the arts, humorist Stephen Leacock published his satire of small-town life, *Sunshine Sketches of a Little Town*, in 1912, and the coterie of artists who would become known as the Group of Seven were working out their unique style in Toronto. Suffragists were campaigning for the women's franchise, while militant workers wanted a fairer share of the proceeds from the new industrial economy. Robert Borden became prime minister following his defeat of Wilfrid Laurier on an anti-free trade platform in the 1911 election. The most contentious political issue facing him was the navy, and whether Canada should even have one. In sum, Canada in 1912 was a country feeling its oats but not quite sure yet how to harness the forces unleashed by industrialism, sudden population growth and prolonged economic expansion. One of these forces was the motor car itself.

After dipping their rear wheels in the Atlantic and collecting some of the water in a flask for delivery to Vancouver, Wilby and Haney departed Halifax on August 27. The first challenge for Haney was to accustom himself to driving on the left-hand side of the road. The rest of North America drove on the right (except for British Columbia), but Nova Scotia would not switch over for another eleven years.

The expedition began after six weeks of steady rain had turned the roads to mud. It was like driving through heavy pancake batter. "It was simply a case of get up early, plow through mud and water all day and go to bed as soon as possible," Haney wrote in his diary.

A Motor Tour Through Canada, despite its breezy title, describes all manner of mishaps and misadventures. Climbing a hill outside of Grand Falls, New Brunswick, the Reo's gas tank ran dry. By blowing into it, Haney managed to force the remaining fumes into the fuel line and kept the engine going until the car crested

F. V. Haney
St. Catharines
Ont.

Diary and Account
for Transcontinental
Trip of the REO.

Across Canada or
Bust

E
D
H186   one
                    1/2

REO

During the expedition Jack Haney kept a daily diary which he titled *Across Canada or Bust* and in which he recorded the duo's misadventures and his growing irritation at the selfishness and snobbery of his travelling companion. The diary survives in B.C.'s provincial archives. The page below describes the first couple of days on the road after leaving Halifax. "Roads were bad. Had much trouble with poor gas and spark plugs. Motor missed all day. Done some cussing." Haney's cryptic entries give an indication of the challenges that lay ahead.

Halifax.
To Vancouver.

8-27. Left Halifax at 4.30 p.m. arrive at Truro 8.00 Bum roads. most of the way. mud got into carburetor. will fix protection for it in the morning. Am so. m tired going to bed now. 10.30 p.m.

8-28. Left Truro at 7.45 got good send off. arrive at moncton 7.30. Roads were bad. Had much trouble with poor gas and spark plugs. motor missed all day. done some cussing. Come near losing spare tires some where near amherst. the bracket got loose. Got a pilot out of amherst. He run out of gas so we left him.

the top of the hill and was able to coast into town. Other hills were too steep to negotiate in low gear so Haney and his rider went up in reverse, sometimes adding the weight of extra passengers for the necessary traction. Corduroy roads made of logs laid crosswise in the mud were a special challenge for the car's primitive suspension. The Reo had to be hauled across streams, through lakes of mud, and out of ditches and sand piles. And that was before things really got bad. At North Bay, Ontario, the road disappeared entirely, so the expedition continued to Sudbury by rail. Beyond Sudbury the road reappeared along the north shore of Lake Huron, though lack of bridges made it necessary to hitch a ride on a tugboat part of the way. After taking three hours to get hauled out of a sinkhole by a team of horses, the Reo pulled into Sault Ste. Marie, twenty days after leaving Halifax, only to discover that the ferry to the Lakehead had left without them.

There was no road across the top of Lake Superior. Local advice was "if you wish to save the car and to arrive at the Pacific with a few pieces of its mechanism still clinging together, keep out of the wilderness of New Ontario. The machine will immolate itself on the first tree stump that blocks the path, or grind itself to junk on the rocks, or drown itself in the swamps and bridgeless rivers." A motorist wishing to drive westward had to dip below the lake into the United States. Wilby knew that any hope of completing an all-Red route purely by road was dashed, but he was determined to stay north of the border anyway. Hitching a ride on a lake freighter, he, Haney and the Reo made the 700 kilometre crossing to Fort William where they discovered there was no road to Manitoba either, so it was back onto the train for the run to Winnipeg.

On the prairies the expedition ran into a new obstacle. Roads were plentiful, but they were composed of fine dirt that turned to a thick, tenacious gumbo in the rain. And it had been raining all summer. It was often safer to avoid the muddy main road and keep to a side trail through the grass. At one point west of Brandon, the

'CROSS
CANADA
WITH THE "ALL
RED" ROUTE REO

travellers wandered into a swamp and the Reo sank up to its axles. With the help of a local pilot, who was along to ensure that this sort of thing didn't happen, they jacked up the car and literally constructed a road out of the slough with wheat sheaves, boulders and brush. On they went, meandering their way along old wagon roads and rutted buffalo trails, following telegraph poles and the rail line so they wouldn't get lost. Every once in a while, Wilby forgot the trials and tribulations of the road and turned his attention to the country through which he was passing. The Cypress Hills moved him to his most lyrical outburst.

The day was superb. A rim of purple-blue hills rimmed the West and flanked us on both sides. Little white houses with red roofs stood out here and there against the blue sky. A long train snaked a line of black across the pinkish earth, and occasionally a badger [actually a gopher] peeped out of his yawning and dangerous burrow in the dun roadway . . . In the short grass we found the ineffaceable eternal trail of the departed monarch – a dark brown line a foot or so wide and several inches deep, running parallel north to south . . . Pencil lines in the vastness of the country, but their very persistence seemed to prove the reality of the Red Man's dream of the buffalo's return. On October 1, Wilby had expected to be in Vancouver; instead, the expedition spent the day crossing southern Alberta, their greatest challenge, the mountain ranges of British Columbia, still ahead.

The Reo crossed the Rockies via the southerly Crowsnest Pass, fighting a stiff headwind. The grades were so steep that Wilby and Haney spent most of the crossing out on the road pushing. Coming down the other side was just as slow; they had to keep stopping to allow the brakes to cool down. The track they followed was narrow and rock strewn and filled with the now-familiar potholes and mud sloughs. It was almost with relief that they saw the road peter out at Yahk and had to resort once again to the railway. This time they just drove the Reo onto the tracks, risking

Following his expedition with Wilby, Jack Haney returned to work at the Reo plant in St. Catharines. In 1914 he married Annie Swan and the couple had two children. Following the war, with the Reo plant shut down, he went to work at Wells Garage. He is shown here, second from the left, at the garage in 1920. He died shortly after his forty-sixth birthday in 1935. His widow Annie was always angry that Wilby received the lion's share of the credit for the duo's cross-Canada expedition.

In Victoria Wilby and Haney were greeted by Attorney General William Bowser, Premier Richard McBride being otherwise occupied. After delivering a letter they had brought from the premier of Manitoba, the two travellers went down to the beach and emptied into the Pacific a bottle of Atlantic seawater they had carried with them from Halifax. The historic moment was captured by Richard Broadbridge, a Vancouver photographer who accompanied the expedition during its visit to the coast. At a banquet that night, A.E. Todd, president of the Victoria Automobile Club, congratulated the travellers on their accomplishment, but because they had not actually driven the whole way, he was unable to confer his gold medal.

"The meeting of the Waters" - Thos. W. Wilby finishing his great journey across Canada by Motor car

Copyright Canada 1912 by R. Broadbridge

This is what the Trans-Canada Highway looked like on Vancouver Island in 1912 when Wilby and Haney arrived. Haney wrote in his account: "We travelled through a veritable forest tunnel of timber, the car dwarfed to insignificance by trees which shot up to the sky and barred the sunlight from spreading banks of fern and flower. The way followed closely the first trail blazed years ago through this solitude and now marked by immense stumps, sooner or later to be torn by dynamite from their anchorages."

that no trains were due from the opposite direction. It was agreed that if a locomotive appeared, they would save themselves by jumping free and sacrifice the car. In the event, they made the three-hour trip to Kitchener, the spot where the road resumed, in great discomfort but without mishap.

The rest of British Columbia passed in a blur of ferry rides, twisting detours, precipitous canyons and near disasters. "We pursued a road that followed the line of least resistance," Wilby wrote, "and took us more often north and south than westward . . . The grades beggar description, and there are sheer drops down to the canyon stream from the narrow ribbon of the road 3,000 feet above sea level which have a knack of getting on the nerves . . ." Along the Fraser River, on a tortuous mountain road after the sun had gone down, the acetylene headlamps ran out of gas. They couldn't stop in the middle of nowhere and there was no point in turning back. Stretching out on his stomach along the car's runningboard, their young guide held an oil lamp close to the edge of the road, which dropped away into a deep canyon. "Inch by inch we crept on," recalled Wilby. "Moment by moment the poor fellow grew stiffer. A sudden jolt and it seemed as if we must throw him down the bank." This went on for fifteen nerve-wracking kilometres until the trio arrived safely at Lytton.

Finally, on October 14, the Reo pulled into Vancouver, "stained with the evidence of strenuous travel, covered with mud and oil and grease" as a reporter for the *Sun* newspaper put it. In a speech at a reception in his honour, Wilby declared that Canada would not be a "true nation" until the Canadian Highway was built, then it was off to Vancouver Island for the official end of the journey at Alberni where the first signpost had been planted five months earlier. But as great as their accomplishment was, Wilby and Haney could not claim the Highway Association's gold medal. They had interrupted their drive at several points with ferry and train rides, and once they had been forced to take a short detour through the United States. The Todd Medal was still up for grabs.

Wilby and Haney collected pennants from many of the communities they visited along the way. When they weren't motoring, they displayed their collection to draw attention to their expedition.

Opposite top: WIlby and Haney stand outside the Customs House in Nanaimo, British Columbia. Members of the Victoria Automobile Club were miffed at this photograph, claiming that the pennants from Alberni and Victoria are hidden behind Haney on the right. They were already angry that the trip was billed as "Halifax to Vancouver," when Vancouver Island was the actual terminus, and they asked that photographs like this one be suppressed.

Opposite bottom: On the other side of the Island the members of the Alberni Board of Trade doff their hats in recognition that the "path-finding journey" has been completed. Note the bottle of Atlantic water resting on the back of the Reo.

"Better roads" was the rallying cry of motorists, especially in western Canada where lack of good roads kept settlers isolated and farmers from their markets. People travelling any distance had to be prepared to build their own roads as they went along. Edmonton auto-mobilists thought the cross-Canada route should follow the Yellowhead Pass across the Rockies, so Charley Niemeyer and Frank Silverthorne set out in June 1922 to show that it could be done. For much of the route they followed the abandoned right-of-way of the Grand Trunk Pacific Railway. Along with 550 kilograms of equipment, they carried four long planks strapped to their Overland vehicle for getting over rough spots. The pair made it to Victoria and won their own medal for doing so. Their sign says "Pathfinding Car Edmonton to Victoria via Jasper and Kamloops."

As Wilby and Haney discovered to their exasperation, in pre-World War One Canada most main highways were surfaced with nothing more than loose gravel, soaked with oil or tar to reduce the dust. In rural areas and on the prairies, basic wagon roads connected farmers to their local markets. Sometimes these roads were graded using a simple drag, a wood frame pulled behind a team of horses. Improvements consisted of filling the most obvious potholes, digging drainage ditches and building up the centre of the roads to encourage runoff. Stretches of corduroy road carried traffic over low, boggy areas, rattling the teeth of passengers and shaking apart their vehicles. Roads were so notoriously bad that new cars came with just a 30-day warranty, their manufacturers recognizing the beating the vehicles would take once they had left the lot. "Macadamizing" of roads had been going on since the mid-19th century but, as transportation historian Edwin Guillet pointed out, this meant little more than covering a dirt surface with loose stone or gravel. Wherever lumber was plentiful, plank roads

presented a convenient alternative. Boards were laid down on stringers, then covered with a dusting of dirt. Paving of urban streets began in the late 19th century, but it was extended to rural roads and highways only piecemeal. Railway building was still the rage, and there was little money left over for good roads. The Canadian Good Roads Association was organized in 1914 to urge highway improvement on all levels of government, but there was no enthusiasm for road-building during the First World War.

One exception was the completion, in 1915, of Ontario's first concrete highway, connecting Toronto and Hamilton. Another was the construction of roads in the national parks by "enemy aliens" who were rounded up and held in internment camps for the duration of the war. The authorities decided that these internees – German and Austro-Hungarian nationals, including Ukrainians, who had been living in Canada – should be put to work. At its peak the internment operation comprised nineteen camps across the country. Near Castle Mountain, in the

"The nightmare of a Liberal senator who helped to throw out the appropriation for good roads." This caricature by political cartoonist Newton McConnell appeared in the *Toronto Daily News* in 1912. The Conservative government of Robert Borden, elected the previous year, had passed road-building legislation, but it was turned back by a Senate dominated by Liberal appointees. It was always convenient for federal politicians who didn't want to spend money to fall back on the argument that roads were a provincial responsibility. The cartoon refers to the fact that Liberal Party leader and former prime minister Wilfrid Laurier could not control his senators.

A group of tourists wheeling along a Rocky Mountain road in 1927. It was visitors like these, eager to see the western mountains, who convinced the federal government that it made sense to put money into highway building in the Rockies following the First World War.

Rockies west of Banff, internees worked on a section of road that would later become part of the Trans-Canada project. Officials were confident that improved access to its scenic wonders would result in a burst of auto tourism in the park. The Castle Mountain camp opened in the summer of 1915 and held about 200 labourers, mainly Ukrainians whose main "crime" seemed to be that they were unemployed and of the wrong nationality. In return for a six-day work week, these men received spartan accommodations in unheated tents and 25 cents a day, much less than free labourers were getting for similar work, or the $1.25 a day being paid to enlisted men, which was supposed to be the standard of comparison for internees, according to the Hague Convention. The project on which they were put to work was the construction of a motor road between Banff and Lake Louise, today one of the most scenic sections along the length of the Trans-Canada Highway. The Castle Mountain internees managed to complete just 12 kilometres of road during two summers of work

before the government closed the camp and dispersed its occupants.

With the return of peace, roadbuilding in general, and the Trans-Canada project in particular, became more of a priority for governments. In 1919, Ottawa established a program of federal grants, while the provinces gradually took over responsibility for roads from the municipalities and began to provide money for construction. With the aim of encouraging public interest, the Canada Motor Association sponsored another cross-country excursion, in the style of Thomas Wilby. This time the vehicle was a brand new Maxwell touring car, the forerunner of the Chrysler in Canada, and the driver was Percy Gomery, president of the Vancouver Auto Club. Accompanying Gomery was his wife, whom in the book he wrote about the trip he insisted on calling "the Skipper". She was probably the first woman to attempt the continental crossing, and modern readers of the book can only wonder how she endured her husband's buffoonish sense of humour for the 32 days it took them to complete the drive.

Tourists appreciated increased road access to the Rocky Mountains, but so did settlers in B.C.'s Columbia Valley who wanted to be able to travel east to Banff and Calgary. One of the road projects they lobbied for was the Banff-Windermere Highway across Vermilion Pass. The B.C. government began construction before the First World War, but when the province ran short of money the federal government stepped in, creating Kootenay National Park in 1920 and completing the road three years later. Today it is Highway 93 and carries motorists between Radium Hot Springs, B.C., and Castle Junction, Alberta. The Kicking Horse Trail was the name given to the highway between Golden, B.C., and Lake Louise, Alberta. Completed by the federal park service in 1928, this stretch was later incorporated into the Trans-Canada system.

Percy Gomery, president of the Vancouver Auto Club, seated at the wheel of his Maxwell touring car. His wife and travelling companion, the Skipper, is nowhere to be seen; perhaps she is taking the photograph. The Maxwell was a popular car until the company fell on hard times during the 1920s. Walter Chrysler took it over, eventually phasing it into his own Chrysler Motor Corp. and ceasing to manufacture the Maxwell. The car lived on in popular culture, however, as the comedian Jack Benny pretended on his radio and television shows to own an old, malfunctioning Maxwell. Note that the steering wheel of Gomery's vehicle is on the "wrong" side. As a resident of British Columbia, Gomery drove on the left-hand side of the road until the province changed over in 1922 to conform to the rest of the country.

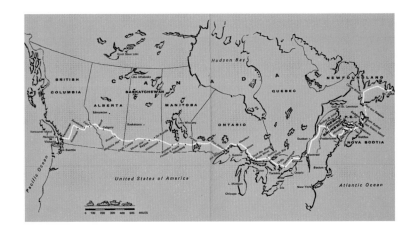

As they left Montreal on June 23, 1920, the Gomerys were already out of the running for the Todd Medal since they chose to begin their trip part way across the country instead of Halifax. Even so, they encountered enough hardship to qualify for a medal of some sort. Eight years since Wilby and Haney, little improvement was visible in the roads of northern Ontario. In his book Gomery describes a harrowing two-day slog along the Ottawa River between Petawawa and Mattawa, a distance of just 90 kilometres. They spent most of the time hunting for the barely-existent road, and the rest hauling themselves over and out of various obstacles. They stopped for lunch at a hotel so isolated from traffic that the owner admitted that the Gomerys were the first automobilists to ever arrive at his door. "Lakes were more common than people," Percy glumly observed. The next day the Maxwell became so hopelessly mired in the mud that Percy had to leave his wife huddled under mosquito netting, armed with an umbrella and a revolver, while he ran several kilometres to the nearest farm-house for help. When he got back with a team of horses, he found "the Skipper" sitting in the car revving the engine to keep away the bears. (Gomery aptly titled this chapter of his book, "Motoring Without Roads".)

The Gomerys lacked the stomach for much more of this, and at Sault Ste. Marie they gladly abandoned Canada for the smoother roads of the northern American states. They recrossed the border through Emerson, Manitoba, and just outside Winnipeg a town constable stopped them for speeding. Gomery refused to pay the fine, pointing out to the magistrate how much bad publicity would fall on his municipality if the cross-Canada excursion was interrupted by jail time. "I'm working for a new Canadian highway which can stand all the publicity it gets," Gomery told the poor magistrate, who smiled gamely and let him go on his way. The Maxwell trundled across the Prairies without further incident, though Gomery described Saskatchewan as the province "where the roads were so cruel and the people so kind." Heading through

During the 1920s traffic congestion emerged as an issue in large Canadian cities. This photo shows Toronto's Yonge Street on a Saturday afternoon in November 1929.

the mountainous interior of southeastern British Columbia, they ran head on into another vehicle high above the Elk River, setting them back $120 in repairs. It would be several years before there was a continuous road across this part of BC, so once again the Gomerys had to dip south of the border where they completed the trip to Vancouver through Washington State. Gomery concluded his account succinctly. "When a public official asked me that night for my outstanding impression of the journey, I said without hesitation; 'How very few people live in this country!'"

Though they shared many similar hair-raising adventures, and many of the same bad roads, a lot had happened between Wilby's epic 1912 trip and the Gomerys' journey. Wilby was an explorer, and just as the early explorers had depended on Native guides to paddle the canoe and find the right path, so Wilby had relied on a hired driver/mechanic and local automobile clubs to guide him through their territory. Gomery and "the Skipper", on the other hand, were more or less on their own. They drove themselves, and

though their trip was sponsored by the Motor Association and was well publicized, they styled themselves "everyday drivers" out for a look at the country. They were, in a word, tourists, and as such were part of the swelling tide of motor travellers that would break over Canada during the 1920s.

IN THE DECADE following the Gomerys' "motor scamper", the number of registered vehicles in Canada tripled, as did government expenditures on roads. The 1920s marks the arrival of "car culture" in Canada. Historian Douglas Owram notes that automobile registrations topped the one million mark and the number of persons per car dropped from 30 to 10. Throughout the decade car registrations climbed by well over 10 percent a year, while the number of horses began to fall for the first time. By 1929, Canada ranked third in the world per capita, after the United States and Hawaii, in automobile ownership. Farmers were behind much of this expansion, demanding improved roads on which to get their produce to

Following the First World War, it became all the rage to attempt long-distance drives in support of highway construction. Usually these excursions were promotions for automobile or parts manufacturers. Bottom: A 1920 Reo Six advertising Maple Leaf tires, headed "from Vancouver to New Brunswick and return." The Reo logo in the background suggests the car is parked outside the company showroom in Vancouver. The car appears to be transporting a dead body on its running board; in fact, the package contains the vast array of tools and spare parts needed by any driver setting off across the country.
Top: A car decorated in support of the highway between Banff and Jasper, which opened in 1940.

By the 1920s provincial governments had been issuing licence plates for several years. In 1921 the issuing authority in B.C. was the provincial policeforce. It mailed each vehicle owner a tab to be affixed to the car's base plate. By 1923 B.C. was issuing a new set of plates annually.

Below:Newfoundland printed the province's name on its plates for the first time in 1926. Only 1,400 plates were issued in Newfoundland that year, compared to more than 300,000 in Ontario.

This 1919 Saskatchewan plate is made of porcelain, commonly used in the early years. Tabs were sent out annually and affixed to the base plate.

Porcelain chipped easily, however, and was expensive to manufacture, so in 1922 Saskatchewan began using metal plates instead.

In some provinces – for example, Ontario and British Columbia – licence plates were manufactured by prison convicts until the 1970s.

As the number of automobiles on Canadian roads increased, so did the regulations controlling their use. Early drivers were required to pin their licences to their lapels while operating their vehicles. By the 1920s it was no longer necessary to have licences plainly visible, but every driver had to pay an annual fee to get one. This B.C. licence was issued to Nellie Mary Jory in 1925 for the cost of one dollar. Regulations varied across the country. In Ontario, for example, motorists didn't require a licence at all prior to 1927. When a driver's licence became mandatory, it could be obtained by simply filling out an application form, without an exam.

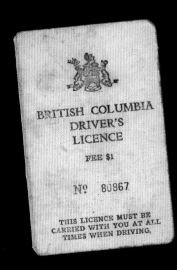

BRITISH COLUMBIA
DRIVER'S
LICENCE

FEE $1

№ 80867

THIS LICENCE MUST BE
CARRIED WITH YOU AT ALL
TIMES WHEN DRIVING.

BRITISH COLUMBIA MOTOR-VEHICLE ACT.

The person named and described hereon and whose signature appears below is hereby licensed to drive or operate any motor-vehicle otherwise than as a chauffeur, upon any highway of this Province.

Name in full *Nellie Mary Jory*

Address *287 62 E Van*

Date *7 Aug 1925* Superintendent Provincial Police

Per *HCBann*
(Signature of issuing official.)

Sex *Female*

_____
(Official position.)

N.M. Jory
(Signature of Licensee.)

Drive **CAREFULLY** and **PRUDENTLY**. You commit an offence when your driving endangers life or property, no matter what your speed may be. Over 20 miles per hour in cities, towns, and villages, and over 30 miles per hour in other places, puts the onus on you of proving yourself innocent of driving to the common danger.

Keep an especial Lookout for Children.

Keep to Extreme Right on Curves.

Use extra Caution in entering or crossing Main Thoroughfares.

Driver on your right has Right-of-way at Intersections.

Make Driving Signals a matter of Habit. Signal about 30 yards before change of direction, and continue Signal till just before turning.

Keep your Brakes in Order. Do it Now. Slack Brakes are Dangerous. Keep your Windshield clean.

Keep your Lights in Order. All of them. Have them properly Focused. Use them at night.

markets. Just as important was the steady
stream of Americans who turned their
vehicles north toward the scenic wonders
of Canada. (Prohibition was in force south
of the border, so many of these visitors
presumably were attracted less by the
scenery than the opportunity to get a
drink.) In 1925, one federal official estimated that two million American-owned
motor cars were entering Canada annually,
accounting for $150 million worth of
tourist spending. No wonder that it was
the needs of American motorists, as much
as their Canadian counterparts, that motivated highway improvements north
of the border. By the mid-1920s, the provinces collectively were spending more on
highways than any other single item in
their budget, and every province had a
good-quality highway connecting it to the
American border. At the same time the
provinces had discovered that automobiles
were a source of revenue. They began im-
posing licence fees on cars and drivers,
and in 1922 Alberta imposed the first
gasoline tax, an innovation that was quickly
adopted by the other provinces. Indeed,

as historian David Monaghan points out,
the rise of the automobile was a contributing factor to the concomitant rise in
the power of provincial governments.

The 1920s have been called "the gold-
en age of motoring" in Canada. "This was
not just a new appliance such as, say, the
electric range," Douglas Owram observes,
"but a new experience." There was still a
sense of adventure in donning one's gog-
gles, leather gauntlets and long, cotton
duster and setting off for a Sunday drive.
Such an elaborate costume was necessary
because motoring was still a dirty business. Roads were dusty in dry weather
and muddy after rain. Early automobiles
had no windshields or side windows and,
until the Twenties, no tops. Driver and
passengers were as exposed to the elements as if they were travelling in an
open carriage. The odds of getting stuck
or breaking down were so high that the
likelihood was that at least some of the
excursion would be spent pushing the
car out of a ditch or walking to a nearby
farm for help. Most motorists did not use
their vehicles in the winter; it was too

The first made-in-Canada "car," Henry Seth Taylor's steam-powered buggy. Note the steam boiler and exhaust pipe behind the driver's seat, and the tiller steering mechanism rather than a steering wheel.

much of a risk to chance bogging down in the snow and freezing to death. Signage was almost non-existent. Road warriors relied on specially prepared guidebooks containing maps and basic directions. There were almost no gas stations or garages. Drivers had to equip themselves with extra petrol and oil and an array of tools and spare parts, and they had to know enough to be their own mechanics.

The resources that went into road building during the Twenties were not matched by a comparable growth in the indigenous Canadian automobile industry. Quite the opposite. After a promising beginning, there was, by the end of the First World War, only one Canadian-owned company manufacturing motor cars. The homegrown industry had enjoyed a brief golden age in the years leading up to the war, then collapsed into bankruptcy and buyout.

The honour of being the first Canadian motorist goes to Father Georges-Antoine Belcourt, who was parish priest at Rustico, Prince Edward Island, when he purchased a steam wagon in Philadelphia and brought it to the island in 1866. This vehicle was

unsuited to local roads and before long the engine was salvaged and used for something else. The very first made-in-Canada motorized vehicle was a steam-powered buggy made in 1867 by Henry Seth Taylor, a watchmaker in Stanstead, Quebec. It crashed because Taylor hadn't thought that brakes were essential. Steam turned out to be a cumbersome technology, useless in winter, when everything froze, and requiring a complicated system to fire up the boiler. By comparison, electricity was simple, clean and effortless. Canada's first electric car was built in Toronto by F.B. Featherstonhaugh and William Still in time for display at the 1893 Canadian National Exhibition. With pneumatic tires and a four horsepower motor, it could travel about 25 kilometres before its batteries needed to be recharged. And therein lay the Achilles heel of the electric car; it had a very limited range. As a result it was the internal combustion engine that eventually prevailed as the motive power of choice for the automobile. The first gas-powered car in Canada was designed and built in 1897

When early motorists ventured beyond the city limits, they came face to face with the lack of good roads and bridges. One advantage of winter driving was that rivers and lakes were frozen, and vehicles could simply drive across them. Once the thaw set in, other solutions had to be improvised.

Top: It was not unusual to rely on a team of horses to haul a stranded motorist out of a slough. These embarrassed excursionists are being rescued near Standard, Alberta, in 1914. Bottom: At Whitecourt, Alberta, in 1939, drivers used a cable set-up to hoist their vehicles across the river during spring breakup.

Before the First World War, the Russell Motor Car Company, a subsidiary of Canada Cycle and Motor (CCM), was one of Canada's "Big Three" auto manufacturers, along with McLaughlin and Ford. Below, a line of Russells parked outside Toronto city hall in 1905. The manufacturer himself, Thomas A. Russell, is seated behind the wheel in the vehicle on the left. While it featured an engine imported from England, the Russell was a Canadian-designed vehicle made by a Canadian-owned company, a rarity at the time. The company motto was "made up to a standard, not down to a price." In 1915 the company was bought by an American manufacturer.

The McKay motor car was manufactured, briefly, by the Nova Scotia Carriage and Motor Car Company, first in Kentville, then in Amherst. In 1912 one of the company founders, Dan McKay, along with his engineer, Archie Pelton, drove from Kentville to Saskatchewan, planning to establish dealerships for their vehicle along the way. Apparently they had no success. Like so many other Canadian automobiles, the McKay was modelled on an American vehicle, the Penn. When that company failed in 1913, the McKay company was left without an American supplier and ceased production.

by Sherbrooke, Quebec, machinist George Foote Foss. His vehicle featured a single-cylinder air-cooled engine with a top speed of close to 20 kilometres an hour. (Always an innovator, Foss later moved to Montreal where he opened the first rapid car-wash operating in the city.)

The motorcars fabricated by Foss and the others were all one-of-a-kind, built by their mechanically-inclined owners and used to trundle around town to the amusement of friends and family. By the turn of the century, however, homemade was giving way to factory production. For the first few years, Canadian manufacturers were among the industry's leaders. The Canada Cycle and Motor Company, more famous as simply CCM, diversified into the auto market in 1905 with the production of the Russell. The Model A Russell was a two-cylinder runabout that sold for $1,300, but the company also manufactured a more powerful, seven-passenger touring car, the Model C, which was considered the premier luxury car in pre-war Canada. Then, at the end of 1915, Russell sold out to Willys-Overland of Ohio. Other domestic manufacturers included the Tudhope Motor Company in Orillia, Ontario, and the Nova Scotia Carriage and Motor Car Company in Kentville, makers of the McKay car. Both of these companies produced a Canadianized version of an American car, and both collapsed when their partners south of the border did, a fate that also befell the only Canadian-owned manufacturer to survive into the Twenties, Gray-Dort Motors. Based in Chatham, Ontario, Gray-Dort produced dependable vehicles at an affordable price that were inexpensive to run. By the early 1920s, there were more Gray-Dorts registered in the prairie provinces than many of the most popular American models, including Dodge and Studebaker. At one point Gray-Dorts outsold the Chevy in Ontario. But the company relied on its American partner, and when U.S. Dort closed in 1925, the Chatham operation followed, ending any hope that a Canadian-owned manufacturer could compete with the large American branch plants.

Gros Morne Mountain, the second-highest peak in Newfoundland, is located in Gros Morne National Park, just off the Trans-Canada on the province's western coast. UNESCO declared the park a World Heritage Site in 1987.

McLaughlin

At the time of the First World War, the Compagnie d'autos de Témiscouata, in Rivière-du-Loup, Quebec, was a typical small-town car dealership that sold cars for the McLaughlin Motor Car Company. Based in Oshawa, Robert McLaughlin manufactured his own version of the Buick and later the Chevrolet. In 1918, the year this photograph was taken, McLaughlin was purchased by General Motors and incorporated as General Motors of Canada.

The two largest foreign-owned manufacturers were General Motors of Canada and Ford of Canada. General Motors began as the McLaughlin Motor Car Company, started by a family of Ontario carriage makers. Under an arrangement with the American auto entrepreneur Will Durant, Sam McLaughlin began making the McLaughlin car with Buick engines at his Oshawa factory in 1908. The company soldiered on until 1918 when McLaughlin sold out to General Motors and became a branch plant, General Motors of Canada. Ford came to Canada when Gordon McGregor, a Walkerville wagon maker, established Ford of Canada in 1904. The U.S. company put up over half of the original capitalization and owned 51 percent of the Canadian operation. Originally, Ford Canada simply brought in parts from across the border and assembled cars at its Walkerville plant. Later it produced Canadian-made Fords. The classic Model T was as popular with Canadian drivers as it was with Americans. It was lightweight, durable and cheap; a 1912 Model T cost $750, and in 1925

a customer could buy a Ford two-seater roadster for as little as $395. Between 1908 and 1927, 750,000 Canadians bought Fords made in Walkerville. (The third of the "Big Three", the Chrysler Corporation, incorporated its Canadian branch plant in 1925.)

With so many people taking to the roads, both tourists and otherwise, service industries emerged to look after their needs. Canada's first gas station opened in 1908 in downtown Vancouver. Motorists pulled up beside the red-brick tank and filled up with a length of garden hose. From this primitive beginning the full-service garage had evolved by the 1920s. As automobile congestion increased, traffic signals and parking lots became a familiar part of the cityscape. Parks and playgrounds became a necessity because streets were no longer safe places for children to play. In a sense, the city had to be redesigned to handle the motor car. Even domestic architecture changed, as garages were added to house the family sedan.

Likewise, roadside facilities appeared to accommodate motor tourists who

In 1904 there were only 535 automobiles driving around Ontario. By 1930 that number had climbed to almost half a million. The car was no longer a luxury; it had become a necessity. Everyone seemed to be living at a quicker pace. This Toronto police officer is manually operating a stop-and-go sign at the intersection of King and Yonge streets. The first traffic lights were introduced in that city in the 1920s. Drivers began to complain of limited parking spots, and pedestrians were warned to refrain from "reckless walking." The motor vehicle had a profound impact on the way Canadians experienced urban life.

Dr. Perry Doolittle (1861–1933) was known as the father of the Trans-Canada Highway for his tireless lobbying in support of a national road. One year he even put a map of the projected route on his

Christmas card. Doolittle, shown at right holding a vehicle spring that he invented, was a founder of the Toronto Automobile Club, which in 1907 helped create the Ontario Motor League.

In 1913 the League (its crest is below) was one of the original members of the Canadian Automobile Association, which Doolittle headed from 1920 until his death.

began to want more in the way of creature comforts than a campsite by the side of the road. In the post-war period, autocamps began to appear, offering a tenting site and basic facilities such as fireplaces, show- ers and laundry. Gradually owners of these camps began to add simple cabins, then more elaborate lodgings. Burton Brown was a typical case. In 1935 he opened a service station at English River on what would be the Trans-Canada in northwestern Ontario. "Everybody who came in for gas, they wanted to know where they could go fishing, "Brown later recalled. "They wanted accommodation to stay overnight so we went into the business of cabins and boats to rent and guides. And we changed the name from Brown's Service Station to Brown's Tourist Camp." As these camps became more elab orate they evolved into the now-familiar motor hotel, or motel. To begin with, these were mom-and-pop operations, like the Browns'. It was not until after the Second World War that large companies began to buy up and operate nationwide chains of motels.

AS THE NUMBER of car owners increased, so did agitation on behalf of the Trans-Canada project. Members of automobile clubs and associations across the country kept up a steady drumbeat of publicity – talking to journalists, publishing road maps, putting up signs and tirelessly lobbying the government. One of the most indefatigable of the automobilists was Dr. Perry Doolittle, a Toronto physician. Doolittle had earned his stripes in the road wars as an advocate for bicyclists in the years before the turn of the century. His 1895 book, *Wheel Outings in Canada,* was a must-read amongst the two-wheel set. Bitten by the motor bug, Doolittle switched his energies to the better roads movement. In 1903, he helped to found the Toronto Automobile Club and for many years he spent his weekends driving around the province nailing road signs onto telegraph poles. He was the first doctor in the city to make house calls by car, and even invented the Doolittle Remountable Rim for changing tires. He was a true enthusiast.

In the fall of 1925, during his long tenure as president of the Canadian

These are licence plate toppers, also known as boosters, from the 1930s. Motorists could attach them to their vehicle plates. The Saskatchewan Motor Club topper is made of aluminum, while the BCAA tag is porcelain. The Milk Transport Association topper was displayed on milk trucks in Toronto.

Doolittle and photographer Ed Flickenger pause in Alberta to capture a stunning picture of the Rocky Mountains. Their 1926 Model T was one of 100,611 units manufactured by Ford in Canada that year. The base price was $395. Ford had sent Doolittle and Flickenger across the country in part to evaluate the impact of the government's support for highway building since federal funding was introduced in 1919. The answer was—discouragingly little. Most roads in Canada still looked like this one: unpaved, potholed, impassable at certain times of the year. The 1925 trip was not Doolittle's last drive across Canada. He did it again in 1931, when he was 70.

Automobile tires took a beating on early roads and weren't expected to last long. A repair kit was necessary for any motorist venturing into the countryside, where roads were strewn with sharp rocks and nails from horses' shoes. At first tires were manufactured perfectly bald; then a non-skid tread was added to increase safety. Firestone, an American company, established a Canadian subsidiary in 1919 and began making tires in Canada three years later. The company road map shows how developed the U.S. road system was — in this case in Michigan — compared to roads in Ontario.

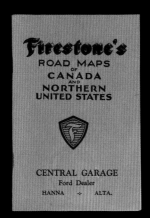

Automobile Association, the gentlemanly Dr. Doolittle embarked on a cross-country drive to promote the national highway. At 64 years of age, he was as tireless as ever. His sponsor was the Ford Motor Company of Canada, celebrating its 21st birthday. Ford provided Doolittle with a Model T fresh off its Windsor assembly line – it was one of the last Model Ts manufactured in Canada; the next year Ford introduced the Model A – and a photographer, Ed Flickenger, to record the trip. The highly-publicized expedition left the shores of the Atlantic at Halifax on September 8 and arrived in Vancouver forty days later. Doolittle and Flickenger managed to average 190 kilometres a day for the entire trip, an exceptional pace compared to earlier crossings. Unlike Wilby and Haney and the Gomerys, they also managed to remain in Canadian territory for the entire trip. But still the Todd Medal went unawarded. It turned out that the Model T's rubber was not always in contact with the road. On several occasions, when Doolittle and Flickenger had run into dead-ends, they exchanged the vehicle's wheels for special steel rims and motored along the railway tracks. Since they travelled a total of 1,365 kilometres in this fashion, they could hardly have been said to have driven across the country.

BECAUSE OF HIS TIRELESS lobbying efforts, posterity has dubbed Perry Doolittle "the father of the Trans-Canada Highway". But when he died in 1933 his dream road remained just that, a dream. Despite the incredible rise in automobile use, governments, and especially the federal government, were slow to respond to the need for better roads. Prime Minister William Lyon Mackenzie King and his Liberal government were stingy about investing in roadbuilding, claiming that they did not wish to interfere in provincial jurisdiction. When a Conservative government came to power in 1930 it endorsed highway construction as a make-work project for the unemployed and that year made federal money available through its Unemployment Relief Act, the first piece of federal legislation to actually mention the "Trans-Canada

Doolittle's Ford was specially designed so that its rubber tires could be replaced with steel flanged rims, allowing it to travel on train tracks. Here it is being converted from road to rail. Because so much of the trip was accomplished by rail, Doolittle and Flickenger did not qualify for the Todd Medal.

North to Alaska

Top: Five months before it opened to traffic, portions of the Alaska Highway were nothing more than logs floating on swamp. Yet the job was completed in record time, and in late November 1942 the first truck convoy reached Fairbanks, Alaska, from the outside world.

Bottom: A fifty-year commemorative postage stamp was issued in 1992. The construction of the highway turned out to be a tragedy for the area's First Nations people, many of whom died of diseases brought into their communities by outsiders building the road.

The most ambitious highway project of the Second-World-War era had nothing to do with the Trans-Canada. It was the Alcan Military Highway, better known as the Alaska Highway, built by American soldiers through Canadian territory in response to the threat of Japanese aggression.

Following the sneak attack by the Japanese air force on Pearl Harbor in December 1941, the U.S. government feared that the enemy might mount an invasion of North America through the Aleutian Islands and the Alaskan mainland. The military decided to build a road across the northeast corner of British Columbia and through Yukon Territory to Fairbanks, Alaska, making the North accessible to soldiers and supplies. With the approval of the Canadian government, more than 11,000 American troops came north in the summer of 1942 to punch through a road. Working seven days a week and long into every night, these soldier/roadbuilders succeeded in clearing a pioneer road across 2,400 kilometres of permafrost, muskeg and mountain ranges. The highway opened to traffic on November 20, 1942.

But that was just the beginning of the job. Now it was the turn of civilian contractors to take the rough track built by the military and turn it into a permanent highway. This work was partially completed by the end of 1943 when, with the Japanese threat no longer imminent, the U.S. government stopped work on the project. By agreement with Ottawa, the Americans continued to manage the road until the end of the war when the section from mile zero at Dawson Creek to the Alaska border was formally handed over to Canada.

British Columbia's Big Bend Highway was one of many stretches of road built to provide jobs for the unemployed during the Great Depression. The Big Bend followed the arc of the Columbia River between Golden and Revelstoke–300 kilometres of driving to travel 80 kilometres as the crow flies.

As the map cover shows, the highway passed through some spectacular mountain scenery. But the winding, unpaved road, barely two lanes wide, was no favourite with drivers, who called it "the world's longest detour." Still, its opening in 1940 meant that motorists could for the first time

drive from Alberta to the coast entirely in Canada. It is significant that when the time came to choose a route for the Trans-Canada through the mountains, engineers recommended against the Big Bend.

Highway" by name. But government money did not necessarily mean rapid construction. So long as the point of the highway project was to provide jobs, there was little incentive to finish it. Projects often were denied heavy equipment, including bulldozers, as efficiency took a back seat to the labour-intensive methods of the pick-and-shovel brigade. Then, as the Great Depression of the 1930s deepened, followed by the outbreak of war, federal money dried up anyway.

Nevertheless, it was during the war that a coast-to-coast through road finally opened. This network of interconnecting provincial roads, more than half of them unpaved and some of them impassable for parts of the year, did not qualify as an official, all-weather Trans-Canada Highway, but it was the next best thing. The final western gap was closed with the completion of the Big Bend Highway linking Golden, BC, with Revelstoke. The Big Bend was a joint project of the British Columbia and federal governments. Construction had begun in the fall of 1929, using money designated

for unemployment relief, but funding cutbacks and the rugged terrain combined to slow progress to a crawl. The pace picked up in 1934 with the passage of the Public Works Construction Act by the federal government. This legislation, part of Prime Minister R.B. Bennett's "New Deal", injected $40 million (the equivalent of $587 million in 2005 dollars) into a variety of public projects, including the Big Bend Highway, which now forged ahead with renewed vigour and was completed in June 1940. At last, motor travel was possible between Alberta and the Pacific Coast on an all-Canadian route. Two years later, in October 1942, road crews in northern Ontario put the finishing touches on a 246-kilometre stretch of gravel road between Hearst and Geraldton. As a result, for the first time a motorist could drive right across the country, without resorting to freighters or train tracks and without having to dip south of the border.

All that remained was for someone to do it, which they did, in 1946. Brigadier R.A. Macfarlane and Kenneth MacGillivray, driving a new Chevrolet, made the

CANADIAN AVIATION
Dominion Among the Leaders in Air Transportation

IN CANADA, because of its vast distances and its rich natural resources in hinterland areas, aviation plays a vital role in transportation. Canada holds a leading position in the movement of air freight and express, and for passengers and mail a network of commercial air lines second to none in efficiency provides swift, regular service.

From St. John's, Newfoundland, on the Atlantic to Victoria, B.C., on the Pacific, Trans-Canada Air Lines, government-owned system, spans the continent, linking most major Canadian cities, and providing service from Toronto to New York, Cleveland and Chicago. Direct air connection from T.C.A. is possible through various air lines to Seattle, Great Falls, Minneapolis, Detroit, Buffalo, New York, Washington and Boston. Regular transatlantic flights to the United Kingdom, begun during the war, are now scheduled, using Department of Transport aircraft operated by T.C.A. Participation is planned in other international air services to

the West Indies and South America, and across the Pacific Ocean to Asia and Australia.

The next largest is Canadian Pacific Air Lines which consolidated in 1942 many independent services. This and many other privately owned air lines provide excellent service, and the famous "bush" pilots stand ready to fly anywhere throughout the country. These charter pilots and other small air services provide the only fast, year-round means of transportation to many mining and lumbering camps and isolated settlements in Canada's great north country. Their skill and daring have "cracked open" regions which were formerly reached only by means of canoe and outboard motor in summer or by tractor train in winter.

Canada is an air-minded country. In two World Wars its brilliant pilots and air crews have blazed a record in the skies that is an inspiration in time of peace. Situated at the crossroads of global air travel, Canada's future in the air is assured.

IMPERIAL DEALER
DOMINION OF CANADA
with Newfoundland & Labrador
Featuring Land, Water, and Air Transportation

LEGEND

Main Highways
(Numbered and numbered)
Principal Winter Tractor Roads
Railway Lines
Steamer Routes
Principal Air Routes

Approximate Time Zones
Royal Canadian Mounted Police Posts
International Boundaries
Provincial Boundaries
District Boundaries

● Principal Airports
● Other Landing Fields
● Principal Seaplane Bases
● Other Seaplane Landings

SCALE OF MILES

IMPERIAL OIL LIMITED

TRANS-CANADA HIGHWAY
First All-Canadian Road Spanning the Dominion from Coast to Coast

FOR YEARS Canadian motorists have dreamed of a continuous automobile road across the continent entirely within the borders of the Dominion. Now that dream is realized with the opening of the final link of the Trans-Canada Highway.

Completion of the 157-mile gap between Hearst and Geraldton, in Northern Ontario, took place in 1943 as a defence measure at a cost of about $6,000,000. Today the Atlantic and Pacific coasts are connected by an all-weather highway that winds east firmly to west, surmounting numerous barriers of mountain, forest, and river.

Varying in width and type of surface—its building was the concern of the various provinces through which it runs rather than of the Dominion government—the highway is improved throughout its 4,108mile length, and long sections are paved.

From its beginning at the rocky shores of the Atlantic Ocean, its course sweeps through a wide variety of country: historic Nova Scotia, old-world Quebec, industrial and agricultural Ontario, across the flat wheatlands of the prairie provinces, the towering ranges of the Rockies, and through great national parks, down the spectacular Fraser Valley, to Vancouver, B.C., on the Pacific Ocean.

Starting at Halifax to Sydney, the road passes successively through Truro and Amherst in Nova Scotia; Moncton, Saint John, Fredericton, and Edmundston in New Brunswick; Rivière du Loup, Quebec, and Montreal in Quebec; Ottawa, North Bay, Cochrane, Port Arthur, and Kenora in Ontario; Winnipeg and Brandon in Manitoba; Regina and Moose Jaw in Saskatchewan; Medicine Hat, Calgary, and Banff in Alberta; and Golden, Revelstoke, Kamloops, Lytton, to Vancouver in British Columbia.

Thousands of miles of highways feed the Trans-Canada Highway, and alternate routes lead the traveller through vast areas of ever-changing beauty.

In New Brunswick a branch winds southward leading to the pastoral province of Prince Edward Island. From Moncton a main trunk follows the jagged east coast of New Brunswick. At the Quebec border the trip may be continued on a circular tour of scenic Gaspé Peninsula. Through Ontario a northerly passage parallels the St. Lawrence River and the shores of Lake Ontario to Toronto and then swings northward through the Muskoka

Lakes region to join the main route at North Bay. From there the motorist may turn toward Sault Ste. Marie, where he may take his car by ferry across Lake Superior to Fort William or Port Arthur. This 250-mile voyage makes an interesting alternative to the long drive through the Northern Ontario forests. Continuing on by way of Kenora and Winnipeg the road leads across the prairies to Medicine Hat as previously described.

Between Medicine Hat, Alberta, and Spences Bridge, B.C., alternate routes offer a variety of attractions. One may take a north-bound course through Lethbridge, Cranbrook, and Trail, skirting the U.S. border; or cross-line northern and southern branches by the Windermere highway from Banff to Cranbrook, or the Okanagan Valley road from Salmon Arm to Penticton.

Eventually, the Ontario section may offer an alternative route along the northern shore of Lake Superior between Sault Ste. Marie and Port Arthur. But whatever route is taken, the cross-to-coast highway—unsurpassed in scenic beauty anywhere.

Along the Highway Near Revelstoke, B.C.

Trans-Canada Highway Near Fredericton, N.B.

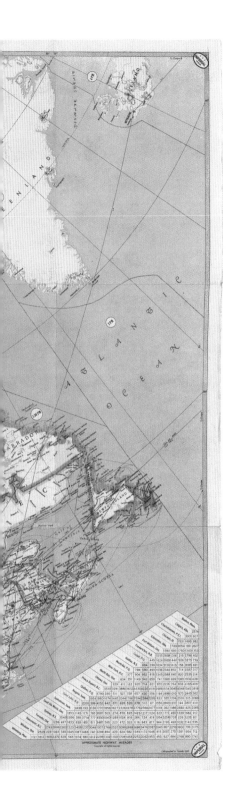

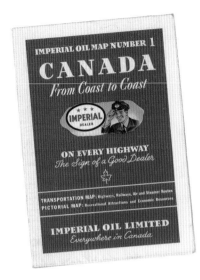

Imperial Oil, Canada's largest petroleum company, issued this map of Canadian transportation routes to commemorate the completion of the road between Hearst and Geraldton, Ontario, the last link in a cross-Canada road system. Imperial has been associated with automobiles in Canada since the first car drove off the assembly line. The company, created in 1880 by a group of refiners in southwestern Ontario, opened the first gas station in the country in 1907, in Vancouver, and began producing road maps for customers in 1935. One of the reasons Imperial, and its gasoline brand Esso, enjoyed such loyalty from Canadian motorists was that from the beginning of television in 1952, the company sponsored the Saturday night hockey broadcasts. In fact, the traditional three-star selection at the end of every hockey game dates back to Imperial's 3 Star gasoline, introduced in 1931.

Plank roads didn't disappear entirely with the advent of modern highways. As late as the 1960s, on this backcountry road in British Columbia's Thompson Valley, planks were laid on steep sections to give vehicles traction on the loose gravel surface.

crossing from Louisbourg, Nova Scotia, to Victoria to claim Todd's medal. (Newfoundland would not join the federation for another three years.) After all the hair-raising adventures of their predecessors, there was something anticlimactic about the ease with which Macfarlane and MacGillivray accomplished their triumph. It took them a mere nine days, and the only reported mishaps were four blown tires. "It is safe to say," Edward McCourt wrote several years later, "that [they] won the medal by default – no one was interested in competing for it."

The fact that it was possible to drive across Canada by car could not disguise the woeful inadequacy of the country's highway system as it emerged from the war. To put it simply, the rapidly expanding number of motor vehicles was outstripping the capacity of the roads to handle them. At the end of the war there were 1.5 million registered cars and trucks in Canada, a figure that would grow by over a million in the next five years. Importantly, almost a quarter of these vehicles belonged to the commercial

fleet and these trucks were becoming not only more numerous but also heavier, requiring better roads built to higher standards. Yet, in 1946, less than four percent of non-urban roads in Canada were hard-surfaced; a surprising 75 percent were still dirt. And of the small percentage that were paved, most of them were in Quebec and Ontario. In the West and in the East, a paved highway was for motorists a rare treat.

It was time to take seriously the need to upgrade Canada's roads and specifically, it was time to dust off the idea of an up-to-date, all-weather highway across the country.

As roads developed, so did the techniques for paving them.

Bottom: In Alexandria, Ontario, a small town between Montreal and Ottawa, a pre–First World War work crew is spreading oil on a layer of crushed rock. The mixture hardened into the typical paved surface of the era.

Top: A 1950s road crew lays pre-mixed asphalt, using a spreader and roller, on a section of the Trans-Canada near North Tryon, Prince Edward Island.

In 1946 someone finally managed to drive a motor vehicle across Canada and claim the Todd Medal. The winners were two veterans of the just-completed war, Brigadier R.A. Macfarlane, who had been in charge of mechanized transport for the Canadian army, and Squadron Leader Kenneth MacGillivray. The pair drove a six-cylinder Chevrolet Stylemaster sedan supplied by General Motors, which exploited the trip in its advertising (below). The duo crossed the country in just nine days, encountering no problems along the way. Their longest day's drive, from North Bay to Fort William, Ontario, was 1,137 kilometres, a respectable distance even by today's standards. The medal, shown in the advertisement, has disappeared.

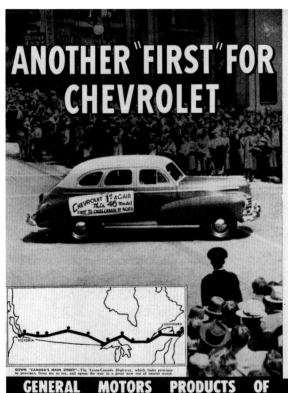

CROSS COUNTRY—Near the end of the road and a medal for making the first transcon tinental auto trip from Nova Scotia to Victoria are Brig. R. A. MacFarlane and Ken Mac Gillivray who arrived in Vancouver Sunday night. They are pictured here at English Bay, getting their first view of the Pacific. Mr. McGillivray is at the left and Jack Cribb, West Coast Salvage and Control Co., Vancouver, a friend, is at the back.

MARATHON AUTO TRIP NEARS END

Two Veterans Make Coast-To-Coast Trip Over Canadian Roads

Two Canadians, travelling across Canada by auto to win a medal donated 34 years ago, ar rived in Vancouver at midnight Sunday and left today for their 5000- mile journey.

Ten days ago Brig. R. A. Mac Farlane, former officer command ing Military District No. 10, and

Squadron Leader Kenneth Mac Gillivray left Louisberg, N.S., with their destination, Victoria, and the prize, a gold medal off ered in 1912 by the late A. E. Todd, of the Capital City.

Mr. Todd, one-time mayor of Victoria, and an active member of the Island Automobile Club, offered the medal for the first motorist to travel across Canada between Louisberg and Victoria in accordance with the rules and route restrictions listed in the regulations for the journey. No time limit was fixed for the drive.

SNOW IN MOUNTAINS

To complete the trip as laid down by Mr. Todd, Brig. MacFar lane and Sqdn. Ldr. MacGillivray must drive over the Island High way, calling at Campbell River and Alberni, before reaching Vic toria.

At Hotel Vancouver today the two travellers reported the roads had been quite passable, although they ran into snow in the B.C. mountains.

Sunday they drove from Grand Forks to Vancouver, a distance of nearly 500 miles.

Their longest day's journey, they reported, was from North Bay to Fort William when they covered 711 miles.

DIES

Thugs Ignore Man's Plea For Mercy

One of two week-end strong arm robbery victims—Paul Cor bell, 1032 East Pender—pleaded with his assailants not to hit him, but was knocked uncon scious. The thugs even removed his shoes in search of loot.

They took $17 from his pock ets.

Corbell said the men followed him from a street car early Sun day.

He pleaded: "Don't hit me; you can have my money," but they struck him in the face and kicked him in the ribs.

Corbell said he got off the car at Tenth and Sasamat, was at tacked at the rear of a friend's home in the 4500 block West Sixteenth. He believed the thugs

MOSCOW, May 20. — (AP)— The Soviet press made no men tion today of reports of fighting between Azerbaijan forces and troops of the Iranian Central

A Vancouver newspaper announces the arrival of Macfarlane and MacGil livray, as well as their departure for Vancouver Island and the last leg of their trans-Canada journey. The challenge laid down in Alberni thirty-four years earlier had finally been met, but there was still much work to be done be fore Canada had a decent transnational highway.

The road through Percé, Quebec.
Quebec was reluctant to sign up for the
Trans-Canada project, but it carried on
a vigorous highway-building program
of its own.

The Road Begins

CHAPTER TWO

*"Our undertaking is the largest East-West construction project
since the building of our Canadian Pacific and Canadian
National Railways."*

Robert Winters, federal Minister of Resources and Development, 1951

ON DECEMBER 10, 1949, the House of
Commons in Ottawa passed An Act to
Encourage and Assist the Construction
of a Trans-Canada Highway. As the title
of the legislation suggested, Ottawa could
not actually build the highway; highways
remained within provincial jurisdiction.
The federal government could only put
some money on the table and broker
an agreement with the provinces. That
turned out to be a much tougher job than
anyone anticipated.

Canada came out of the Second World
War riding a wave of prosperity. In 1946
there were only 163,000 people unemployed, just over three percent of the
labour force. The inflation rate was low,
the value of farm products was high and
consumer spending was rising steadily.
The first planks of the welfare state had
been put in place with the introduction of
an unemployment insurance scheme in
1940 and the family allowance in 1944.
At war's end there was even talk of a national health insurance program. On the
other hand, Mackenzie King's government, while accepting that the state had

a role to play in managing the economy,
expected the private sector to spearhead
post-war reconstruction. Large public
works projects, the Trans-Canada Highway being one, would stay on the shelf, to
be brought down and implemented only
in the event of an economic downturn.

Relations between Ottawa and the
provinces at this point were cranky. Both
George Drew, the Conservative premier
of Ontario, and Maurice Duplessis,
the nationalist leader of Quebec, were
staunch defenders of provincial rights,
loud in their denunciation of what they
took to be incursions into provincial
jurisdiction. During the wartime emergency, the provinces had ceded control
of personal and corporate taxation to the
federal government to pay war costs. In
return for lost revenue, the provinces
received an annual subsidy. After the
war Ottawa proposed continuing this
arrangement to finance conversion back
to a peacetime economy and to pay for its
new social programs. But Quebec and
Ontario would not agree. In the end
Ottawa made "tax rental" agreements with

The post-war future of the Trans-Canada Highway was intimately connected to wartime politics. As this drawing by Halifax editorial cartoonist Bob Chambers indicates, although Prime Minister Mackenzie King managed to navigate the crisis over conscription, the affair left Quebec disaffected with the federal government and left King reluctant to engage in another issue, such as the highway, that would alienate the French-speaking province even more.

only seven of the nine provinces. (King's successor as prime minister, Louis St. Laurent, resolved the differences with Ontario in 1950 and with Quebec in 1954.) This dickering over tax policy was an indicator of the troubles that lay ahead when the governments turned their attention to the Trans-Canada Highway.

Despite the obvious need for better roads, King was reluctant to get involved in the highway project. This was chiefly because of Quebec. The province was still seething from the wartime conscription battle. In April 1942 King had put conscription to a national referendum, asking voters to release him from his pledge not to introduce compulsory service. In Quebec the referendum result was 72.9 percent against conscription, while in the rest of Canada 80 percent of voters said yes. Just as King had feared, the country was divided, French against English. The prime minister hoped against hope that he would not have to use the mandate the referendum gave him to invoke conscription, but finally, in November 1944, as personnel short-

ages in the Canadian army reached crisis proportions, King announced a call-up. In the end fewer than thirteen thousand conscripts went overseas, but the issue drove a bitter wedge between English- and French-speaking Canadians.

King, as well as St. Laurent, who succeeded him in 1948, had no desire to poke another stick at the Quebec lion by forcing the highway issue. But pressure on the government began to mount. Several provincial premiers lobbied strenuously in favour of the project. They viewed a national highway as a source of jobs, a promoter of tourism and an important investment in the economic infrastructure of the country. At the federal Liberal convention in 1948, delegates voted to make completion of the highway part of the party platform, more or less forcing the government at least to appear to be doing something about it. As a result, in December 1948 Ottawa convened the first federal-provincial meeting to discuss the project. To no one's surprise, Quebec stayed away, citing the "constitutional problem," but the other provinces

As the politicians dragged their feet, the country suddenly grew wider with Newfoundland's decision to join Canada. The vote was held in July 1948, and these Islanders in Corner Brook are reading the results in the press.

Bottom: Prime Minister Louis St. Laurent, in front of the main entrance to the Parliament Buildings in Ottawa, speaks at the official ceremony welcoming Newfoundland into Confederation. Former prime minister Mackenzie King is seated far right.

Seated between them is F. Gordon Bradley, a prominent supporter of Confederation and Newfoundland's first representative in the federal cabinet.

moved ahead with planning during 1949. On March 31, 1949, as plans for a national highway were taking shape, Newfoundland joined Canada as the tenth province, abruptly adding another 980 kilometres to the highway project.

Initially Prime Minister St. Laurent insisted that all the provinces had to be party to any agreement, but eventually he agreed to proceed with as many as could be mustered. Historian David Monaghan argues that finally it was the fear of unemployment that got the federal government moving. Monaghan believes that Ottawa always considered the highway a make-work project, so when economic forecasters predicted a significant increase in jobless numbers in the near future, the St. Laurent government gave the project a green light. Late in October 1949 the *Trans-Canada Highway Act* was tabled in the House of Commons.

THE ACT that passed through Parliament on December 10, 1949, by no means resolved all differences of opinion between Ottawa and the provinces. As the Toronto magazine *Saturday Night* pointed out, "the project bristles with difficulties and conflicting interests." First of all, the act proposed a cost-sharing arrangement that would see the federal government pay half the cost of construction. Ottawa also agreed to pay one hundred percent of the cost of roads built through national parks and to compensate the provinces for half the cost of all highways built before 1949 that became part of the Trans-Canada system. Some provinces were unhappy with this formula, suggesting that Ottawa should pay more. British Columbia even wanted Ottawa to pay for everything. Second of all, the act specified only that the highway would follow "the shortest practicable route," and there was a great deal of disagreement about what that route should be. And lastly, Quebec would not sign on, arguing that any federal control over routes or technical specifications was an unacceptable violation of provincial sovereignty.

The cabinet minister chiefly responsible for resolving these problems was Robert Winters, minister of reconstruction

The route the new highway would follow as it crossed the country was a contentious issue. Most hoped the road would pass through their community. In British Columbia residents of Nelson rallied to promote the advantages of a route across the "sunny southern" portion of the province.

On September 10, 1948, they organized an "On to Nelson" caravan of cars in support of a southern route through the mountains. As it turned out, engineers chose a more northerly route, across Rogers Pass.

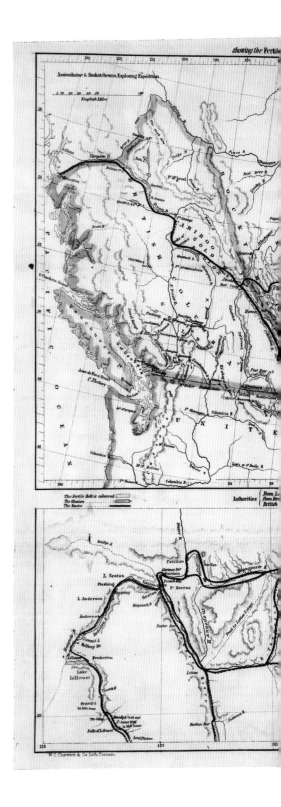

In the 1920s, when this photo was taken in British Columbia's Okanagan Valley, country roads followed a path of least resistance. Speed was not so important, since automobiles of the era could not go very fast anyway. Instead, motorists followed circuitous routes to get from here to there.

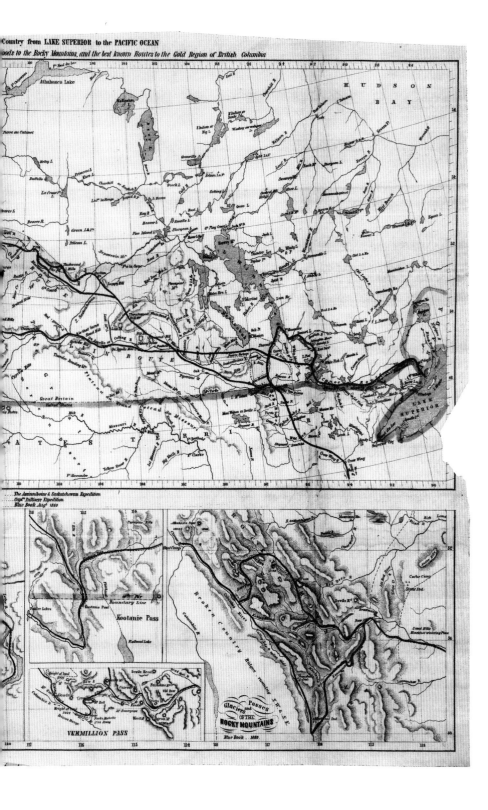

Finding the best transportation routes across Canada was a challenge faced by generations of explorers, traders and surveyors. This map, drawn by Henry Youle Hind, dates back to 1862. Hind, a geologist, accompanied two government expeditions to explore western Canada and assess its potential as a settlement frontier. His map identified some of the same mountain passes that later surveyors would consider when locating a route for the Trans-Canada.

Cabinet minister Robert Winters (shown here behind the microphone) led the federal government delegation at the signing of the Trans-Canada Highway Agreement. Winters, a Nova Scotia engineer turned politician, had been given the job of obtaining provincial support for the agreement. It was a bit like herding cats. The initial meeting of government representatives to discuss the highway project had taken place in Ottawa in December 1948. As the newspaper article at right explains, it was "just barely possible" to drive across Canada by that time, though it was neither easy nor safe to do so. The provinces welcomed the federal offer to fund half the cost of a national highway, but they had various reservations about the plan, and it took several years of negotiation before they all signed on.

and supply, later minister of public works. Winters was an engineer from Nova Scotia who had served in the army during the war and was first elected to Parliament from his native Lunenburg in 1945. He joined the cabinet in 1948 as a protege of the powerful minister of trade and commerce, C.D. Howe. Winters recognized that he would not be able to get all the provinces to sign on to the highway agreement, but he was prepared to make a deal with any that were willing to participate. This meant that initially only six of the ten provinces endorsed the project. Quebec, Nova Scotia, New Brunswick and Newfoundland would have to be convinced.

The reluctant eastern provinces were unhappy with the construction standards Ottawa wanted to impose on them. For reasons of conformity, safety and durability, federal officials wanted uniform specifications across the country. The highway's paved surface would be between 6.7 and 7.3 metres (22-24 feet), with unpaved shoulders extending another 3 metres (10 feet) on either side. The asphalt, spread over a gravel base, had to be at least 76 millimetres (3 inches) thick. To accommodate heavy trucks, hills could not exceed 6 degrees of elevation, and motorists had to be able to see at least 183 metres (600 feet) down the road ahead of them at all times. What these standards meant for the provinces was that many of the existing roads they intended to incorporate into the Trans-Canada network would have to be widened and improved, at their expense. (Alone among the Atlantic provinces, Prince Edward Island showed no reluctance to join the project, the promise of improved highway connections to its mainland neighbours outweighing any doubts about standards.)

The route issue was equally contentious. Most everyone agreed that the road should run as close to the U.S. border as possible to give easy access to American tourists and to compete for commercial truckers' business with existing transport routes south of the border. After that, agreement ended. Nova Scotia and New Brunswick wanted the road to pass through their major population centres.

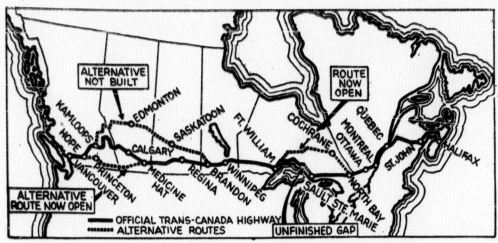

TRANS-CANADA HIGHWAY PLANS will bring the premiers of nine provinces or their representatives to Ottawa next week at the invitation of the Department of Mines and Resources. Map shows the official route and alternative routes now in existence or being considered. Only gap in the official route is along the north shore of Lake Superior.

TRANS-CANADA ROAD TALKS SET

Defence Department Interested in Highway

OTTAWA (CP)—First steps will be taken here next week toward plans for a Trans-Canada Highway, and the Federal cabinet is reported to be still considering what financial inducements it will offer the provinces.

All nine provinces have accepted the Dominion Government's invitation to participate in the talks and it is believed here that the provincial premiers themselves will come to Ottawa to take part in the discussions. The meetings open Dec. 14.

While Resources Minister MacKinnon's department is sponsoring the conference, other Federal groups are interested as well. The Defence Department is expected to have representatives at the meetings who will be interested not only in the route of the highway but in its construction specifications, because of the road's military value.

The Federal Government's share in the cost of the project is expected to run into many millions of dollars, but the question of sharing of the cost will be only one phase of the opening meetings. One of the major topics will be the route of the highway.

At present it is possible—but just barely possible—to travel the 4,300 miles from Halifax to Vancouver by road through Canada. However, sections through the Rockies, the Prairies and northwestern Ontario are particularly bad.

Latest figures available from the Dominion Bureau of Statistics show that during the 25 years ended 1946, Canada added an average of 5,200 miles a year to her network of highways. However, not all of this was surfaced road. Of 553,000 miles of highway in Canada at the end of 1946, only some 140,049 miles were surfaced.

Some idea of the cost of road building and maintenance also is shown in the DBS report. During 1946 alone, an estimated $144,469,000 was spent by various authorities — an increase of nearly 72 per cent over the 1945 total of $84,165,000.

Provincial outlays climbed from $73,536,000 in 1945 to $126,611,000, with construction up $44,300,000. Dominion expenditures, due mainly to the taking over of the Alaska Highway in April, 1946, from the United States, rose from $1,073,581 to $6,293,419. Municipal expenditures also were heavier, increasing from $9,441,779 to $11,266,811.

Roses Bloom In City Snow

Roses in December is more than the title of a tune to Mrs.

Ex-King Peter To Tour Canada

NEW YORK (AP) — Former King Peter of Yugoslavia said

Big Muddy badlands
in south central
Saskatchewan.

A fixed link between Cape Breton and mainland Nova Scotia was talked about for many years, but it was not until Newfoundland joined Canada in 1949 that the discussions got serious. Planners opted for a causeway because of concerns that a bridge could not withstand the high winds, ice and severe winter weather.

Most of the rock used to build the Canso Causeway came from nearby Cape Porcupine, where it was blasted and hauled to the site by truck. Tunnels were drilled into the rock face and packed with dynamite. Each explosion brought down 120,000 tonnes of rock.

For Nova Scotia, that meant the capital of Halifax, while New Brunswick wanted a route that included the business capital of Saint John. But this would mean adding costly detours to the most direct route, and Winters refused. New Brunswick gave in and signed on to the highway agreement in 1950. Nova Scotia held out for two more years, but ultimately signed on when the federal government agreed to build the Canso Causeway.

Of all the stretches of road built as part of the new highway, none had been so avidly anticipated as the causeway across the Strait of Canso. The strait, a deep, narrow channel 27 kilometres long, separates mainland Nova Scotia from Cape Breton Island. With the coming of the railway, a ferry service had been inaugurated across the strait, but as Cape Breton developed as a coal-mining and industrial centre, the inadequacy of the ferry, and the isolation of the island, became more apparent. With Newfoundland's entry into Confederation in 1949, traffic was expected to increase. A fixed link was needed, but for years engineers

and politicians could not decide whether it should be a bridge or some other permanent crossing. Finally it was agreed that a causeway was the most suitable, cost-effective structure.

The federal government began construction of the causeway in September 1952. Rock was blasted out of the granite face of nearby Cape Porcupine, then trucked to the water's edge, where it was dumped into the strait. At its base on the ocean floor, the S-shaped causeway is 262 metres wide (860 feet), tapering to 24.5 metres (80 feet) on the surface. A kilometre in length, it consists of 10 million tonnes of rock and cost about $22 million to build ($165 million in 2005 dollars). It is the deepest causeway in the world. A navigation lock and bridge at one end allows ships to pass through the strait.

The Canso Causeway opened to traffic with much fanfare on August 13, 1955. An estimated forty thousand people turned up to watch C.D. Howe cut the ribbon. For the first time Cape Breton had a reliable all-weather link to the Canadian mainland. Over the next few years Port

Celebrants gather to listen to the speeches at the opening ceremony for the Canso Causeway on August 13, 1955. C.D. Howe was on hand to represent the federal government and cut the ceremonial ribbon.

Hawkesbury and Mulgrave, the communities at either end of the causeway, flourished as ice-free ports. A pulp mill, a quarry, a gypsum plant and an oil refinery all set up nearby. The development the causeway brought to the region seemed to justify optimistic predictions that the Trans-Canada Highway would bring important benefits to the communities it passed through.

Meanwhile, in Ontario the projected route of the new highway was causing the same problems it had in the Atlantic provinces. Federal officials wanted a northerly road running from Ottawa up the Ottawa River valley to North Bay, and on to the head of Lake Superior via Kirkland Lake and Hearst before heading off to Manitoba. This may have been the direct route across Ontario, but it skirted the most populated parts of the province, which were in the south, and thus did little for local motorists or American tourists. The province dug in its heels and Ottawa gave in, agreeing to a more southerly route through Peterborough, close to Toronto, before turning north

toward Sudbury, Sault Ste. Marie and the north shore of Lake Superior. This route was longer and required much new construction, but it made more sense for Ontario motorists.

THE TRANS-CANADA HIGHWAY was one of several projects initiated by a country feeling the flush of prosperity and brimming with optimism. The project was in large part a response to the incredible increase in automobile use in Canada, which in turn was made possible by the good times of the post-war era. More Canadians had more disposable income to buy a car and hit the highway. At the onset of the Depression there had been over a million cars registered in Canada, making the country, per capita, second only to the United States as the car-craziest nation in the world. But during the 1930s car registration declined, as fewer people could afford vehicles in hard economic times. Then, during the war, other manufacturing priorities took precedence over automobiles. In 1941 the government decided that no more civilian cars should

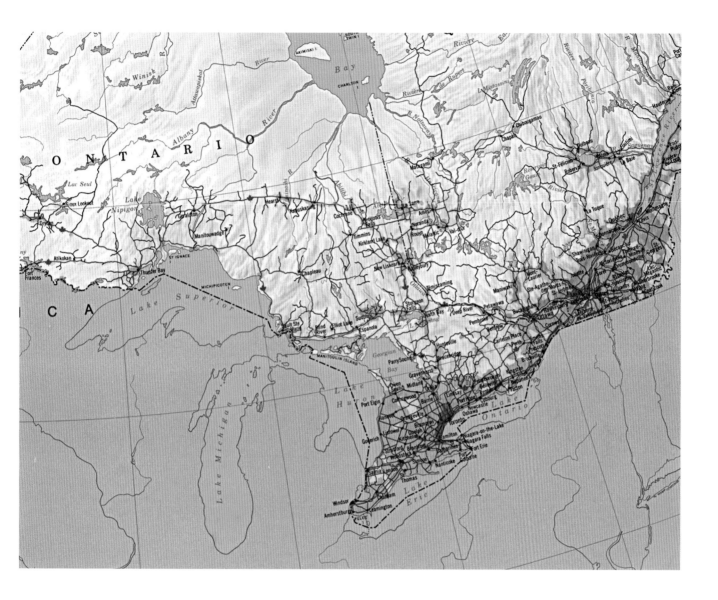

This map shows the dense network of highways in southern Ontario and Quebec by 1981. It also shows the difference between the straightest route across the country and a route that passes through the main population centres. Federal government planners preferred the former; the provinces preferred the latter. The result was often a compromise.

By 1942 it dawned on authorities that they were wasting metal by issuing a set of licence plates each year, similar to the set from P.E.I. shown below.

Ontario (top left) issued a sticker for motorists to display in their windshield. Manitoba (bottom left) switched to an annual tab that could be attached to the base plate. Quebec (bottom middle) began

producing masonite plates instead of metal. As for Newfoundland (bottom right), the numbers on this 1945 plate were hand-painted to save production costs.

be produced for the duration of the war. Manufacturers used their plants for military vehicles instead. Gasoline and tires were rationed; parts disappeared from stores. To show their patriotism, many Canadians simply put their cars up on blocks until peace broke out.

As a result, once the war was over there was a pent-up demand waiting to be met. For the first time in years Canadians were free to take to the highways. Between 1945 and 1952 the number of cars on Canadian roads doubled. By 1960 two-thirds of all Canadian households owned a car, and one in ten were two-car families.

This dramatic increase in automobile ownership was connected to the rise of the suburbs. In the fifteen years following the war, more than a million Canadians moved to the suburbs. The period saw the emergence of a new urban landscape: a central core surrounded by expanding neighbourhoods distant from the town centre. The single-family detached home with a yard of its own became the housing ideal for most Canadians. The symbol of this suburban dream was the shopping

mall, a collection of stores surrounded by hectares of paved parking lot. And it was all made possible by "the great god CAR," as historian Arthur Lower called it in his 1958 book, *Canadians in the Making.* "A patient, obedient god who takes you where you want to go, faster than any magic carpet. A comfortable, well-upholstered god. A god whose priests well know how to gain new worshippers by playing on the qualities of vulgarity and ostentation. And, above all, the god of power, who multiplied man's ego manifold. Yet a ruthless god, sometimes, too, who could turn on his idolater and rend him." By that last comment, Lower was no doubt referring to the fact that the number of deaths and injuries from car accidents was increasing every year.

By the 1950s the automobile had become for most Canadians a symbol of the good life. It represented prosperity and mobility. It promised speed and annihilated distance. Cars made the country accessible in a way it had not been before. And what cars they were. Whether you wanted a family station wagon or a sporty

During the Second World War, Canadians parked their cars to conserve gas, tires and other items that were rationed during the conflict. These Toronto-area residents are walking to work as a contribution to the war effort. Gasoline was strictly rationed, except for essential use. Doctors, for example, were exempt from the restrictions, and farmers were permitted to buy coloured gasoline for use in farm equipment only. Ration books were issued, and anyone found in violation of the regulations faced fines up to $5,000.

American car designers in the 1950s stressed the power and grace associated with airplanes and spaceships. Everything from hubcaps to hood ornaments was designed to enhance the automobile's sleek dynamism. Above, a selection of hood ornaments from the mid-1950s.

two-seater, the 1950s was a decade of exuberance and excess in automobile design. Each autumn the public greeted with anticipation the unveiling of the next year's most extravagant models. It was the beginning of the space age, and automobiles took on some of the appearance of small rocket ships, with swooping tail fins (introduced on the 1948 Cadillac), bulbous chrome hubcaps and ornate radiator grills. And the colours – cars sported two- and three-tone paint jobs in every shade of the rainbow. Safety and economy took a back seat to speed and flamboyance as cars got longer, flashier and more powerful. "The dinosaur in the driveway," one auto executive called the modern American automobile.

The pinnacle of this trend seemed to come at the end of the decade when Ford, with much fanfare, launched the notorious Edsel for the 1958 model year. With its "teletouch" power transmission (push buttons placed in the centre of the steering wheel) and its distinctive "horse-collar" grille, the Edsel represented the triumph of style over function. And it

turned out to be the most embarrassing failure in the history of the American auto industry. Production stopped after just three years as automakers absorbed the fact that consumers were beginning to want less expensive, smaller, more fuel-efficient vehicles. The result was the first generation of American-made compact cars. Still, automobiles continued to be designed more for looks than safety or performance, a point driven home in Ralph Nader's crusading 1965 book, *Unsafe at Any Speed.*

IN 1953 the federal government asked the National Film Board to make a documentary about the Trans-Canada Highway project, titled *Canada's New Main Street,* and people began referring to the road as the country's "main street." In any community the main street is where people come together to share news about what's going on. It is also the most important commercial thoroughfare – the place where people obtain the necessities of life, whether they be groceries, a haircut, a library book or a roll of binder twine.

The Edsel was named for Henry Ford's son after a long search for an alternative moniker. Ford's marketing department even asked the poet Marianne Moore to make some suggestions.

Among the names she came up with were Silver Sword, Pastelogram and Utopian Turtletop. After that, Edsel must have sounded pretty good.

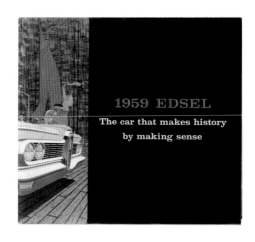

In the 1950s American-made cars featured ornate styling and lots of chrome, as these brochures for the Pontiac and the Edsel illustrate. The Edsel was a spectacular failure when it was introduced for the 1958 model year. It was even launched with its own television special, *The Edsel Show,* but sales were disappointing. Unluckily for Ford, the new car's arrival coincided with an economic recession. Consumers were moving away from big luxury vehicles toward lower-price compacts.

A&W was Canada's first roadside burger chain, opening in Winnipeg in 1956. The novelty of curbside cuisine attracted media attention. Within ten years, the franchise had multiplied to over 200 drive-in restaurants, serving the fascination of the Baby Boomer generation and their parents with the cult of the car. Some A&W's featured carhops on rollerskates, gliding with full trays among the tailfins.

Fast Cars, Fast Food

The automobile epitomized the new, affluent consumer culture. North Americans wanted to put their wealth on display, and what better way to do so than to tool around town in a flashy gas guzzler. What's more, car culture created a demand for its own forms of "drive-in" entertainment. Cars had become a second skin that no one wanted to shed, even for a moment.

The drive-in restaurant provided a place where automobilists could eat in their cars from trays delivered straight from the kitchen by uniformed "carhops." In Canada this concept was pioneered by a Vancouver entrepreneur named Nat Bailey. In 1928 Bailey opened the first White Spot drive-in restaurant in south Vancouver. He borrowed the name from a California burger joint and featured a menu of "barbecued sandwiches" and cold drinks. The White Spot chain eventually became as symbolic of Vancouver as wet weather and the North Shore mountains.

Credit for building the first national chain of drive-in restaurants belongs to A&W. Named for Roy Allen and Frank Wright, the American root beer sellers who pioneered the concept, A&W arrived in Canada in 1956, when the first drive-in operation opened in Winnipeg, featuring a menu of burgers, french fries and, of course, the ubiquitous root beer. By 1966 driers looking for a Mama Burger could pull into any of the more than 200 A&W outlets across the country. Eventually, as labour costs became an issue, A&W and its competitors replaced "drive-in" with "drive-thru" and the carhop went the way of the hula hoop and the poodle skirt.

Peters' Drive-In has been part of the Calgary car culture for more than forty years. Famous for its milkshakes, it still draws crowds to its location on the Trans-Canada Highway. Bridal parties get fed for free – it's a tradition.

Promoters of the Trans-Canada expected it to become the main commercial thoroughfare of Canada, allowing goods to be hauled by truck and trailer from one end of the country to the other. Trucks were more flexible than trains, heading wherever they needed to go at any time of the day or night. Communities without a road connection to the outside world were at a serious disadvantage, and they knew it. People were so desperate to have roads that they would build them themselves if they had no alternative.

Take the town of Nakina in northern Ontario. For years there was no road out of town. Motorists could drive to the town limits, but no farther. To go south they had to freight their cars by rail seventy-five kilometres to Longlac and the nearest highway. In 1953, exasperated at the long wait for a road, the people of Nakina began to build their own, using borrowed equipment and unpaid labour. The result was Ontario Highway 584. The same desperation drove the residents of the Chilcotin Plateau in central British Columbia, where the provincial government had decided it was just

too expensive and too difficult to provide a highway. As a result, the people built it themselves. In 1953 they completed a 450-kilometre stretch, most of it unpaved, crossing their plateau from the Fraser River to the Pacific Ocean at Bella Coola.

By 1950 trucks accounted for almost twenty-five percent of all vehicle registrations in Canada, a substantial increase since before the war. The war had given a boost to trucking, showing that in an emergency, trucks provided versatile service, even though gas and tires were rationed and fleets had a hard time finding drivers with so many men going into the Forces. The industry had been battling the railways for years, but the fact was that many small communities relied completely on trucks to haul their goods, and they did so without government subsidy. The federal government helped things along by lifting the ban on trucking through national parks in 1950.

The Trans-Canada project was a recognition of the vital importance of roads to the national economy. As transportation historian Edwin Guillet observed, "What

In post-war Ontario, the provincial department of highways tried to prevent flat tires by deploying this curious piece of equipment, the magnetic nail picker. During the summer it cruised the province, removing nails and other metal objects from major roads. The machinery consisted of two electro-magnets, powered by a gas motor, hanging off the back of the truck.

Lake O'Hara in Yoho National Park. The Trans-Canada Highway passes through the park.

The official opening of the Trans-Canada in 1962 renewed public enthusiasm for a project that had been many years in the making. Among the items produced to commemorate the completion was a Trans-Canada bridge-building set for youngsters.

> *"What the waterways were in the century before Confederation, what the railways were in most of the century that followed, roads are today – the arteries which feed Canada's industry and commerce."*
>
> Edwin Guillet, federal Minister of Resources and Development, 1951

historian Edwin Guillet observed, "What the waterways were in the century before Confederation, what the railways were in most of the century that followed, roads are today – the arteries which feed Canada's industry and commerce." Guillet wrote that in 1967, and his words are even more true today, when seventy-five percent of total spending on freight transportation in Canada is for shipping by truck. In 2000 more than six hundred thousand large trucks (over 4.5 tonnes)were registered in Canada, and most of them hauled their cargoes along the national highway. The Trans-Canada has fulfilled its creators' dreams that it would become a commercial "main street" for Canada.

THE TRANS-CANADA was one of the many projects initiated by the most successful government in Canadian history. Thanks to the disaster of the Great Depression, William Lyon Mackenzie King led his Liberal party back to power in Ottawa in 1935, and it would be 22 years before they were dislodged. That was the longest unbroken stretch that any federal party had

held power for in the country, and King himself was the longest-serving prime minister in any British dominion. During this time Canada emerged from its worst economic crisis and survived a terrible war to enjoy its most sustained period of prosperity. A series of ambitious government projects dates back to this heady period of Liberal hegemony. Along with the Trans-Canada Highway, there was the St. Lawrence Seaway, the system of locks and canals linking Montreal and Lake Ontario, which began construction in 1954; the Canada Council for the Arts, created in 1957; the Distant Early Warning (DEW) Line of 22 radar stations across the north to defend against Soviet bomber attack; and further extension of the welfare state.

However, all things come to an end. It only seemed as if the Liberals would govern forever. Instead of renewing the party, an aging St. Laurent – he was seventy-four in 1956 – clung to power, and voters began to find him and his party complacent and arrogant.

The immediate issue that contributed

to the Liberals' downfall was yet another national construction project, the Trans-Canada Pipeline. One of C.D. Howe's pet projects, the pipeline was meant to carry natural gas from wells in Alberta to consumers in central Canada. The government wanted the pipeline to travel through Canadian territory and to be built by private interests, albeit with public subsidy. The issue became highly controversial. Some argued that the government should build the line itself; others objected to the substantial involvement of American financiers in the pipeline syndicate. The required legislation came to Parliament early in May 1956, and the Liberals wanted quick passage so that construction could begin that summer. Debate was rowdy and sustained. Opposition was led by the Co-operative Commonwealth Federation (CCF) member from Winnipeg, Stanley Knowles, a master manipulator of parliamentary procedure who thwarted the government at every step. The House Speaker, René Beaudoin, was unequal to the task of managing the situation, and Parliament descended into

When the Trans-Canada
Highway Agreement was
signed in 1949, participants
thought the project would
be completed in seven
years. This chart shows
where things stood in
1956: less than a third was
complete. Furthermore,
Quebec had still not
signed on to the project,
though the Quebec gov-
ernment was engaged in
extensive highway build-
ing in the province.

PROVINCE	AMOUNT GRADED	AMOUNT PAVED	LENGTH OF TCH BY PROVINCE
Newfoundland	347.0	0	981.6
Nova Scotia	51.5	30.2	498.8
Prince Edward Island	88.5	84.3	119.1
New Brunswick	106.2	95.9	624.4
Ontario	669.5	564.2	2,272.3
Manitoba	244.6	247.2	490.8
Saskatchewan	590.6	491.3	666.2
Alberta	344.5	315.6	469.9
British Columbia	329.0	285.3	1,113.6
National Parks	41.8	9.3	113.6
Total kilometres	**2,817.2**	**2,122.7**	**7,350.6**

each other. The climax came on so-called
"Black Friday," June 1, when the session
dissolved into pandemonium and members had to be restrained from assaulting
each other. Finally the government invoked
closure, shutting off debate and passing
the legislation.

In the subsequent election campaign,
opposition parties were able to portray
the Liberals as high-handed dictators,
riding roughshod over the rights of Parliament and remaining out of touch with
ordinary people. On June 10, 1957, John
Diefenbaker led his Conservative party to
an upset victory at the polls. For the first
time since the middle of the Depression,
Canadians had chosen someone other
than the Liberals to run their government.

AGAINST THIS BACKDROP of a faltering
national government, the Trans-Canada
Highway ran into troubles of its own. The
initial highway agreement between Ottawa
and the provinces expired on March 31,
1956. Overly optimistic officials had expected the project would be completed by
that time, but Canada's second national

dream was looking more and more like
an impossible dream. As the deadline
neared, less than half the job was finished.
More than 4,000 kilometres of the route
were not completed to standard, and 518
kilometres were simply not driveable at
all. None of the Newfoundland section
was paved. As well, the total cost of the
project, which had been estimated at
$300 million, was well over budget.

There were good reasons for the delay,
which went beyond the usual bureaucratic
sluggishness. First of all, construction
had not got underway promptly in 1949,
at least not in the provinces that delayed
signing the agreement. It was no surprise that in those provinces the project
was behind schedule. Elsewhere, route
changes added years to the project. In
British Columbia the Big Bend route was
abandoned in favour of the shorter route
through Rogers Pass. This required new
surveys, and the change was not con-
firmed until early in 1956. As well, in the
early 1950s, strategic materials such as
steel and cement were redirected to the
Korean War effort.

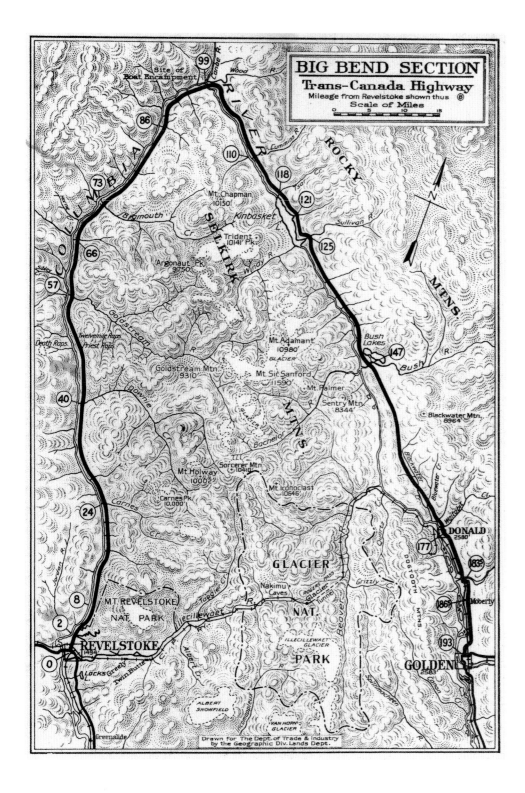

One thing delaying completion of the highway through British Columbia was the decision to build a new road through Rogers Pass instead of using the existing Big Bend route. In 1952 the federal government had asked a group of engineers to research the best route through the Selkirk Mountains. The experts evaluated five different routes and concluded that Rogers Pass showed the most promise. The provincial government could hardly have objected – the adopted route passed through two national parks, Glacier and Revelstoke, meaning Ottawa paid one hundred percent of the building costs.

Traffic congestion was a growing problem in post-war Canada. This clogged artery lies outside Toronto, as thousands of cars creep fender to fender, seeking the great open spaces on a summer afternoon in 1948. One solution was the Queen Elizabeth Way (QEW), Canada's first superhighway. Running from Toronto to Niagara Falls, it was officially opened on June 7, 1939, by Queen Elizabeth, consort of King George VI, and improved and extended in later years. The photograph above shows a stretch of the QEW near St. Catharines in 1950. It represented everything that supporters of the Trans-Canada hoped for in a national highway.

The public grew tired of what it perceived as government inaction on a number of pressing issues, including construction of a national highway. Editorial cartoonist John Collins reflected this frustration in his 1950 caricature "Our New National Anthem." A trio of politicians harmonize on a lullaby for voters: "Oh, we mustn't be daring, we mustn't be bold, maybe we'll do something before you are old."

Most importantly, the Trans-Canada project took a back seat to other roads the provinces considered a higher priority. During the 1950s provincial spending on roads and highways increased dramatically in an attempt to keep up with the skyrocketing increase in motor vehicle use. But most of this money went to build and maintain roads in and around major urban centres, not to the Trans-Canada. Traffic congestion in the cities, where more than half of all automotive traffic was concentrated, was seen to be the more pressing problem. Take Ontario as an example, where the big challenge was to keep traffic moving in and around Toronto and between Toronto and the American border. The Queen Elizabeth Way, Canada's first four-lane, controlled-access superhighway, opened in 1939, but it was not completed between Toronto and Fort Erie until 1956. North of Toronto's downtown, Highway 401 was completed that same year as a bypass across the top of the city, but it was inadequate almost before it was finished and engineers immediately set to work planning its expansion. These costly urban projects, and similar undertakings in the other provinces, siphoned away money that could have gone to the completion of the Trans-Canada.

Despite these excuses, the public was losing patience with what looked like government foot-dragging over the highway construction. Typical was this comment from an editorial in Vancouver's *Province* newspaper on October 17, 1955: "The shameful record of our one transcontinental highway, which should be a lifeline to our whole economy, is a blot on the story of Canadian progress." The goverment's own engineers were warning that as things stood, the project would not be completed for at least another fifteen years. Something had to be done to break the logjam.

The Cariboo Road

The Cariboo Road was British Columbia's first highway to the interior, and the route up the Fraser River Canyon chosen by road builders almost 150 years ago still forms an important link in the Trans-Canada chain.

With the discovery of gold in the central interior of British Columbia in the early 1860s, the region known as the Cariboo was flooded with prospectors looking to make the big strike. Governor James Douglas decided to build a wagon road to the gold camps so that supplies could be hauled in, gold could be hauled out and his authority could be extended over the miners. Work on the road began in 1862 at Yale, which was as far up the river as steamboats could travel from the coast. Most of the southern section had to be blasted out of the Fraser Canyon's sheer rock walls. The job was finished in the summer of 1865 when the road, 5.5 metres wide and 492 kilometres long, reached Barkerville, the capital of the goldfields.

During the 1880s the Canadian Pacific Railway chose to follow the canyon route through the interior and plunked its main line down on top of the Cariboo Road. With the appearance of the automobile, roadbuilders reclaimed the route, and during the 1920s the new Fraser Canyon Highway was built, once again linking the Lower Mainland by road to the central interior. It is this stretch of highway, rebuilt and upgraded, that today carries the Trans-Canada through the stunning grandeur of the Fraser Canyon.

The Fraser Canyon through central British Columbia presented incredible challenges to highway builders as far back as the colonial era. Opposite: The Alexandra Bridge carries the highway across the Fraser north of Yale.

The original Cariboo Road snakes around China Bar Bluff forty-five kilometres north of Yale.

Traffic slows to a crawl as it passes through a section of the Fraser Canyon under construction in the 1950s.

The Fraser corridor was not the only difficult section through B.C. Above, a bridge carries the early highway across the raging Kicking Horse River in Yoho National Park.

CHAPTER THREE

Miles to Go

"In Canada there is too much of everything. Too much rock, too much prairie, too much tundra, too much mountain, too much forest."

Edward McCourt, *The Road Across Canada*

FACED WITH A PROJECT that threatened to go on forever, Robert Winters would have agreed with the writer Ed McCourt's assessment of the country. The public works minister was being challenged from all corners to do something to get the highway on track. It was unthinkable for his government to simply walk away from the half-completed job. The only alternative seemed to be more money, and a new agreement with the provinces.

Discussions began in the fall of 1955. Winters came up with a new offer of federal funds, what became known as his "90/10 formula". He was addressing the fact that some provinces were not proceeding with new construction through their most rugged terrain because it was so costly. Under the terms of the new formula, Ottawa would continue to pay half of all new construction costs, but it would increase its contribution to 90 percent for the most difficult ten percent of the road in each province. The provinces had their own complaints, arguing that when all expenses were factored in, the federal share of construction so far was

closer to 40 percent than half. There is no question that provincial budgets were feeling the strain of paying for the 1950s boom in road construction. Newfoundland, for instance, was devoting almost 40 percent of its revenues to roads, while in Saskatchewan the figure approached a quarter. Winters made some concessions to these concerns and a deal was struck. In April 1956, Parliament amended the highway act, extending it for another four years and kicking in another $100 million of federal money, raising Ottawa's stake in the project to $250 million. The highway had its second wind.

GIVEN ITS FLAT TERRAIN, it was no surprise that Saskatchewan was the first province to complete construction of its portion of the highway. Sixteen months after the federal-provincial agreement was extended, on August 21, 1957, Premier Tommy Douglas used a pair of silver scissors to snip a ribbon completing the Regina bypass and opening the 650-kilometre stretch of highway across his province to traffic. Actually, the politicians

This map from the Atlas of Canada shows the status of major Canadian roads as of 1955, the year before the Trans-Canada Highway Agreement was renegotiated. Most of the roads are provincial highways, but the map highlights the portions of the Trans-Canada that were completed by then. No portion is shown for Quebec, which was not yet a party to the agreement. The map also features a table showing road distances between major Canadian centres.

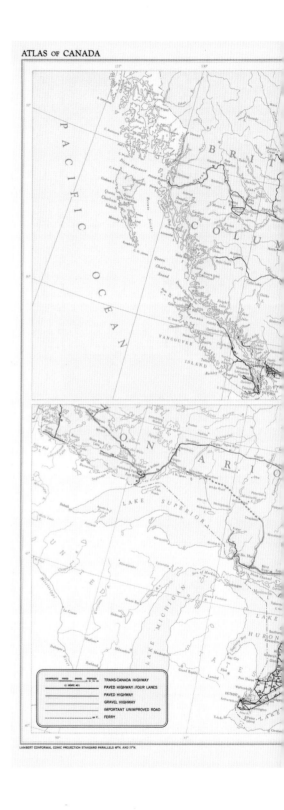

Near Wawa, Ont., the open road beckons. When it opened to traffic in 1960, this stretch of highway completed the Trans-Canada across Ontario.

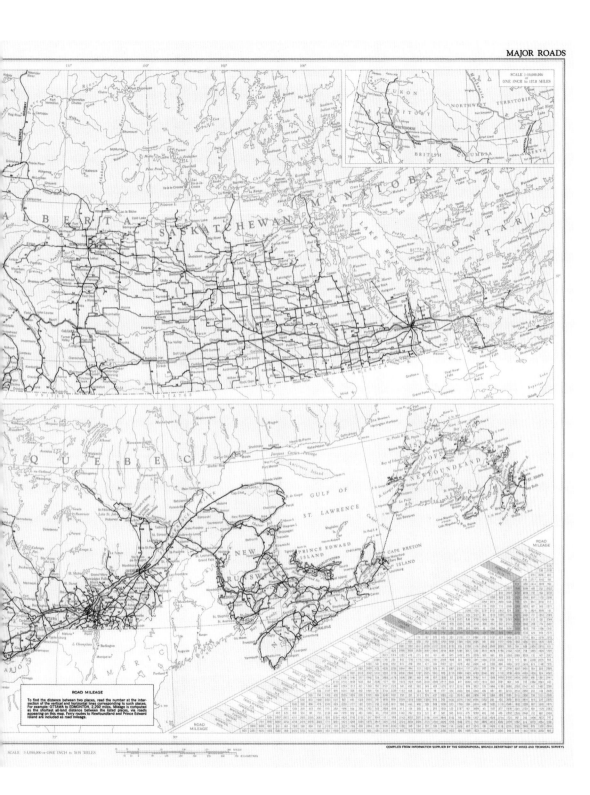

ROAD MILEAGE

To find the distance between two places, read the number at the intersection of the vertical and horizontal lines corresponding to such places. For example: OTTAWA to EDMONTON, 2,292 miles. Mileage is computed as the shortest all-land distance between the listed places, via roads appearing on this map. Ferry routes to Newfoundland and Prince Edward Island are included as road mileage.

SCALE 1:5,090,000 or ONE INCH to 78.91 MILES

COMPILED FROM INFORMATION SUPPLIED BY THE GEOGRAPHICAL BRANCH, DEPARTMENT OF MINES AND TECHNICAL SURVEYS

had jumped the gun. There was still a bit of paving left to finish that fall, so it was actually the last day of October before the job was done. At noon on the last day of the month, crews laid down the final stretch of hardtop. Two hours later the winter's first blizzard arrived, freezing the ground solid. If they hadn't finished, it would have been the next spring before work could resume. With just minutes to spare, it was one province down, nine to go.

QUEBEC, MEANWHILE, was still outside the deal. Under Premier Maurice Duplessis, the champion of provincial autonomy, *la belle province* had never signed the Trans-Canada agreement. Road improvements had surged ahead – Quebecers were as fond of their cars as anyone else in Canada – but not as part of the national network. Only with the death of Duplessis in 1959, and the re-surgence of the provincial Liberal Party under the new, federalist premier Jean Lesage, did cooperative ventures like the Trans-Canada become a possibility.

In 1960, Quebec belatedly joined the agreement, the last province to do so. As part of the deal, Quebec was promised a brand new bridge spanning the St. Lawrence River to carry the highway into Montreal. That promise evolved into the Louis-Hippolyte-LaFontaine Bridge-Tunnel, one of the most innovative of the many crossings along the Trans-Canada. The bridge portion from the south shore to an island in the middle of the river was straightforward enough, but the decision to carry the highway the rest of the way into the city via a tunnel presented a challenge to engineers. They couldn't dig through the thick mud of the river bottom, nor could they bore through the deep bedrock. The solution was a unique, pre-cast concrete tunnel. Sections were fabricated on land, then floated out onto the river and sunk, piece by piece, into an underwater trench. Once in position the sections were joined and the tunnel was done. Along with the Montreal subway, the massive power dams in the north and several other large construction projects, the LaFontaine bridge-tunnel exemplified

Top: The control room is the nerve centre of the bridge-tunnel, featuring the state-of-the-art technology that characterized Quebec.

Bottom: Traffic enters the tunnel portion of the Louis-Hippolyte-Lafontaine Bridge-Tunnel under the St. Lawrence River in Montreal.

The highway winds its way up into the hills just north of Kenny Lake, Ontario, near MacGregor Cove in Lake Superior Provincial Park. This was one of the most isolated, challenging sections of the highway for builders.

the spirit of innovation and expansion that were the hallmarks of Quebec's Quiet Revolution of the 1960s.

As WORK on the Trans-Canada accelerated all across the country, it became clear that there were two sections that presented special challenges to engineers. One of these was a particularly ornery stretch of rough country north of Sault Ste Marie across the top of Lake Superior. There had never been a road through this part of Ontario, home to the Anishinabe (Ojibway) people. Fur traders had found their way here by canoe; latterly it was accessible only by water, rail or floatplane. Motorists travelling between southern Ontario and Manitoba had to follow a route below Lake Superior through the United States. It is easy to see how the stark beauty of this landscape with its fiery fall colours inspired the Group of Seven to produce some of their finest paintings. But for roadbuilders, it was hell. Lengthy stretches of solid Precambrian rock gave way every now and then to patches of boggy muskeg deep enough

to swallow a bulldozer whole, and thick stands of timber that had never seen an axe. Along with twenty-five rivers, the road crosses one lake, White Lake, where an unusual stabilizing arch bridge had to be built, itself costing $1.2 million.

Construction crews set to work closing this gap at Agawa Bay on the eastern shore of Superior, 145 km north of the Sault. The first step was to chop a 46-metre-wide right-of-way through the bush. Field camps were established along the route, and men, equipment and supplies were flown in or taken by boat and barge. The section north of Agawa – the name is an Anishinabe word for "sacred place" – cost close to $200,000 per kilometre as crews had to blast a wide trench through solid rock. In total it took 1.36 million kilograms (3 million pounds) of explosives to clear the right-of-way. The muskeg, which in places was three metres deep, had to be filled with rock, sand and gravel, whatever provided a solid base for pavement. On one occasion a three-kilometre stretch of newly-paved road was swallowed up completely by the muskeg overnight.

Top: A blaster plants some dynamite in a hole while building the right-of-way for Highway 11 through central Ontario in 1917. Note the lack of hard hat or other safety equipment.

Bottom: By the 1950s, workers relied less on explosives and more on jackhammers and earth-moving equipment. This is a section of the Trans-Canada between Bigwood and Rutter, Ontario, in August 1953.

Crews worked year-round, enduring the blistering heat of summer and the frigid cold of winter. Spring brought the relief of warmer temperatures, but it also heralded the arrival of blackflies and mosquitoes. Insect repellant became the roadbuilder's best friend.

Perhaps the only consolation for the 3,200 workers and engineers who planned and built the road was that ten years earlier it would have been worse. During the 1950s there had been a steady improvement in the size and manoeuvrability of earth-moving equipment: graders, bulldozers and trucks. Probably the most important innovation was the use of large pneumatic tires, sometimes up to three metres in diameter, which made the heavy graders and lifters easier to jockey around the worksite. Pneumatic compactors replaced old-fashioned steamrollers; dump trucks the size of small houses distributed huge loads of fill. All of this meant economies of scale for the contractors and some relief for the pick-and-shovel brigade.

"The Gap", as this 272-kilometre stretch between Agawa Bay and Marathon had come to be known, was officially closed on September 17, 1960 when officials gathered in the rain at the mining town of Wawa to declare the highway open. *The Globe and Mail* headline read, WAWA ROARS IN RAIN AS ROAD OVER ROCKS OPENS NORTHERN BUSH. A line of 4,000 automobiles waited to be among the first to drive the new road. The significance of the project to Ontario and to the Trans-Canada Highway as a whole was indicated by the presence at the ceremony of the federal minister of transport, George Hees (Robert Winters had gone down to defeat with so many other Liberals in the electoral debacle of 1957), along with Ontario premier Leslie Frost and no less than five of his cabinet ministers. It had taken four years to complete the job, at a cost of $40 million, but it meant that Ontario's 2,325-kilometre portion of the Trans-Canada was done. To commemorate the opening the town installed a giant plaster-and-wire statue of a Canada goose beside the road, Wawa being an Anishinabe word for wild goose. The original monument actually talked;

Following the war, construction methods improved steadily, much to the relief of the men who built the roads. The photograph above shows a crew working on a highway right-of-way in Simcoe County, Ontario, in the 1920s. No machinery is evident. Rock was broken up using muscle power, then loaded onto flats and hauled from the site by horses.

Opposite: Men work on the Port Mann Bridge across the Fraser River. When it opened in 1964, the bridge carried the Trans-Canada from the Fraser Valley into the suburbs of Vancouver, a section known today as the "Gateway to the Lower Mainland."

Pooh Bear from Canada

The Wawa goose is not the only roadside animal in this section of the Trans-Canada. Ninety kilometres farther north, at White River, stands a marbelite statue of Winnie the Pooh, sitting in a tree clutching his honey pot. This beloved storybook character, adapted by Walt Disney, was based on an actual bear that hailed from this part of Ontario. In 1914, Lt. Harry Colebourn, a Canadian army veterinarian, was riding the train east on his way overseas to join the fighting. On the station platform at White River, he met a hunter who had killed a mother black bear and was selling her cub for $20. Colebourn bought the cub, named it Winnipeg after his hometown, and took it to England as the mascot for his 2nd Canadian Infantry Brigade. When the brigade received orders to ship out for the front, he gave the cub to the London Zoo for safekeeping. Winnie, as the bear became known, was a favourite with visitors to the zoo, among them the writer A.A. Milne and his young son Christopher. Later, Milne incorporated Winnie into the character of Winnie-the-Pooh, "the bear of little brain." Winnie died at the zoo in 1934.

The Winnie-the-Pooh stories, illustrated by E.H. Shepard, have been favourites with young readers since they first appeared in 1926. Not many Canadian youngsters know that Pooh was based on an Ontario bear. The statue of Winnie at White River, Ontario, is one of many monuments that line the Trans-Canada. Another is the giant Canada goose at Wawa, erected upon completion of the final section of the highway through Ontario.

The Big Bend Highway through eastern British Columbia was unpaved. For much of the route, motorists drove through kilometre after kilometre of dense cedar forest.

visitors could press a button and the bird gave its own history. But it did not withstand the winter weather and was replaced in 1963 by a steel bird, standing 8.5 metres tall and weighing two tonnes.

The completion of The Gap left one major roadblock remaining: Rogers Pass in the Selkirk Mountains of Glacier National Park. Rogers Pass itself had been discovered by, and named for, the eccentric surveyor, Major Albert Rogers, while he was locating a route through the mountains for the Canadian Pacific mainline. During the summer of 1885, CP work crews pushed the line up and over the pass, braving mudslides, forest fires and avalanches to reach Craigellachie, west of Revelstoke, where the last spike was driven that November. The pass turned out to be a constant peril to train traffic, chiefly from the snow which thundered down across the track from the surrounding slopes. Snowsheds were built to protect the line, but they could not resist the worst slides. In March, 1910, a crew was working to clear a train blocked in the pass when an avalanche swept

down on them, killing 62 men, still the single worst railway accident in the country's history. Following that incident Canadian Pacific built the eight-kilometre-long Connaught Tunnel, then the longest tunnel in North America, and with its completion in 1916 the railway was able to avoid Rogers Pass by going under it.

When it came time to build the first roads through the mountains, engineers considered a route through the pass to be too difficult. By 1927, drivers could reach Yoho National Park from the east, and Revelstoke from the west, but the gap between remained impassable. To close it, engineers chose an indirect route that followed the big bend of the Columbia River north from Revelstoke then south again to Golden in an arc that stretched for 305 kilometres. Built as a Depression-era make-work project, the Big Bend Highway opened in June 1940. At last motor vehicles could travel an all-Canadian route between Alberta and the Pacific Coast, though it took seven hours to drive the perilous gravel road and very few motorists or truckers could be bothered

Mountain driving has
always had its challenges,
avalanches being chief
among them. It soon
became clear that when
snow thundered down the
surrounding slopes, the
highway could be impassa-
ble for weeks. One answer
was to excavate a tunnel
through the hard-packed
snow. Photographer
Byron Harmon took
this photograph in Yoho
National Park. Harmon,
a photographer based in
Banff during the first half
of the twentieth century,
specialized in scenic shots
of the Rocky Mountains.

In 1949 Topps Chewing Gum began selling licence plate trading cards with its gum. By 1953 a complete set consisted of 75 different cards, including plates from the Canadian provinces, the American states and several foreign countries. The colourful cards were not exact replicas of the real plates, but they were close.

On the reverse side of the Topps trading card was information about the particular province, state or country, along with a question – in this case, name the provincial capital. When the card was held up to a mirror, the correct answer was revealed. Topps was not the only company to take advantage of the public's fascination with automobiles. In the mid-1950s, General Mills gave away small metal licence plate replicas in every box of Wheaties breakfast cereal.

to do it. That was where things stood until 1962 when the new Trans-Canada Highway shaved about five hours off the Revelstoke-Golden drive and restored Rogers Pass as the preeminent route through the interior mountains.

The decision to route the highway across the pass, elevation 1,323 metres, was taken in 1956, but it took the next six years to get the job done. The challenges of the Rogers Pass section were many. The site was isolated. Weather was unpredictable. Terrain was steep, crisscrossed by deep gorges and prone to landslides. Workers got used to blasting a stretch of right-of-way only to have it buried under a new pile of rubble cascading down from the slopes above.

When they couldn't go through the rock they had to go around it, on occasion hanging the highway off the side of the mountain. Compared to the flat prairie, where crews could build a kilometre and a half of road in a week, in the mountains progress was slowed to just a few metres a day. The pass receives an average of 8.5 metres of snow a year, so ways had to

be found to protect the highway from the avalanches that had proven such a deadly threat to the railway. First of all, workers scattered "dragon's teeth" across the face of the most dangerous slopes, large, cone-shaped mounds of concrete designed to impede the flow of snow as it tumbled down the mountainside. The highway itself was protected by high earth embankments and a series of snowsheds – concrete and steel tunnels over the roadway with thick roofs reinforced with tonnes of stone. As well there were eighteen artillery emplacements through the pass, used to shell the snowfields to create small avalanches before a dangerous amount of snow had accumulated. (Originally the dynamite was pre-planted and set off, when required, by remote control; however, local bears kept eating the explosives.) These howitzers were, and still are, fired by members of the Royal Canadian Horse Artillery under the direction of forecasters who study snowpack conditions with the aid of remote sensors. When motorists stop at the summit of Rogers Pass to admire the spectacular

Top left: Workers carve out a section of the Big Bend Highway high above the Columbia River. The interior of British Columbia is rippled with high mountain ranges and steep river canyons. Much of the highway had to be constructed on ledges barely wide enough to hold a tractor, under the threat of mud and rock slides.

Top right: Heavy equipment is at work on the Fraser Canyon section of the Trans-Canada near Hell's Gate in 1952.

Opposite: Rogers Pass was the final link in the completion of the Trans-Canada. For modern motorists it is a worry-free drive, thanks to the latest in avalanche control technology. But during the thirty years that the Canadian Pacific Railway used the pass (1885–1916), 250 workers lost their lives trying to keep the line open.

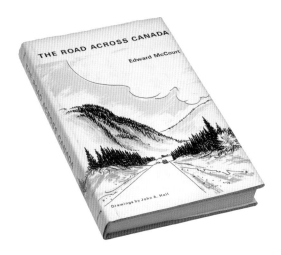

mountain scenery, most of them do not even realize that they are protected by one of the most sophisticated avalanche control systems in the world.

THE ROGERS PASS section of the Trans-Canada cost about a million dollars a mile to build. With its official opening on September 3, 1962 by Prime Minister Diefenbaker, the national highway was complete. It was estimated to have taken 20 million man-days to build. And with its completion a challenge was posed to Canadians: Get out and discover the country. Canada was accessible as never before. The road was ready. There seemed to be no reason for Canadians not to launch themselves across it.

In the summer of 1963, when the highway was less than a year old, Edward McCourt, a professor of literature at the University of Saskatchewan, and his wife, Margaret, took up the challenge. Captivated by the idea of discovering their own country by driving across it, the McCourts loaded up the family sedan and headed for Newfoundland, where, from atop

Signal Hill overlooking St. John's harbour, they flung themselves westward toward the setting sun.

The McCourts were pioneers. A few years later it would become a rite of passage to get out on the open road. The shoulders of the Trans-Canada would be crowded with long-haired hitchhikers in tie-dyed t-shirts and love beads. For these young vagabonds, the highway represented freedom, adventure. But the McCourts were ahead of their time. The Canada through which they drove that summer had not yet tumbled over the brink into social upheaval. They did not know that the complacent Fifties were about to explode into the psychedelic Sixties. That the baby boom generation was ready to embark on an era of sex, drugs and rock 'n roll. That in Quebec, the Quiet Revolution was about to get very noisy. The assassination of American president John F. Kennedy, the escalation of the fighting in Vietnam, the arrival of the Beatles in North America – all were still a year away. Woodstock was just a sleepy little town in upstate New York.

Early drivers were expected to find their own way through the slowly improving network of country roads, often with the help of a guide produced by an automobile club. A big step forward occurred in 1920 when Arthur "Ace" Emmett, a founder of the Winnipeg Automobile Club, came up with the idea of identifying main roads by giving them numbers. The provincial government agreed to implement the plan if Emmett could sell it to the general public, so he spent the next year travelling around Manitoba explaining his system. Emmett's idea was incorporated into Manitoba's Good Roads Act and was copied by other jurisdictions on both sides of the border. Next came proper road maps, which the provinces began issuing in the 1930s. The map from Quebec dates from 1932 and is among the earliest.

Quebec 1932

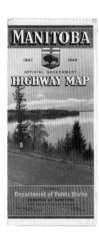

Manitoba 1947

Alberta 1951

Ontario 1962

Looking back, it was an Age of Innocence, not yet an Age of Aquarius.

But it didn't seem so at the time. The ten years leading up to the country's centennial was one of the most turbulent decades in Canada's political history. For one thing it featured the bitter struggle for power between the Conservative Party leader John Diefenbaker and the Liberals' Lester Pearson. Voters couldn't seem to decide between the jowly Prairie populist and the bland Eastern academic. The result was five federal elections and four minority governments in ten years. But the changes that were transforming Canadian society went far deeper than politics. It was an era of isms: feminism, separatism, bilingualism, nationalism, environmentalism, even, in Quebec, terrorism. Because of the baby boom, Canada was a young country again; almost half the population was under 25 years of age. At the same time it was still riding the post-war wave of economic prosperity that had brought an improved living standard for most Canadians. People, and governments, were full of optimism

that they could change the world for the better. Their efforts took many forms, whether it was hippies living communally in the backwoods of British Columbia; or the Saskatchewan government introducing a medical insurance scheme that would later be used as the model for a nationwide medicare system; or a federal royal commission affirming that Canada was a bilingual, bicultural country. At all levels of government and in every corner of the country, change was in the air. There was even a new flag, signifying an end to the old, solemn, "British" Canada and the birth of an exuberant, proudly independent spirit.

ASIDE FROM THE SCENERY, the greatest distraction for drivers negotiating the highway in the summer of 1963 were the work crews hurrying to put the final touches on the road that the politicians had declared finished a year earlier. As Ed McCourt and his wife found out to their discomfort, hundreds of kilometres remained unpaved and under construction. In the book that he wrote about their

Michel Pellegrim and Josianne Masseau ask for a lift on the Trans-Canada near Brandon, Manitoba, in the summer of 1998. The pair, heading from Quebec to the west coast, are part of a long procession of young people who have used the highway as a way of finding out about the country. Almost as soon as the Trans-Canada was completed in the 1960s, hitchhiking across it became a rite of passage for young adventurers.

> *"The Trans-Canada Highway emerges with shocking suddenness from the forest of the Laurentian Shield on to the limitless prairie. The sky billows out to twice its former size; eyes accustomed for many hundreds of miles to looking down a tunnel are unblinkered, and the horizon slips away to a point so remote that it is hard to say where earth ends and sky begins."*
>
> Edward McCourt, *The Road Across Canada*

All along their way, the McCourts came across work crews hurrying to put the finishing touches on the highway the politicians had declared finished a year earlier. This crew is paving east of English River, Ontario.

trip, Professor McCourt described the "dense clouds of dust hanging over the road for miles, through which monstrous trucks and cats [tractors] bore down upon us with terrifying speed; roller-coaster forest trails hardly more than one-way tracks; blind hills and paralyzing right-angle curves." That was in Newfoundland, but it could have been any of many unfinished stretches along the way.

In many ways the McCourts resembled the earliest travellers who had crossed the country by canoe and wagon so many years before. They set off in the same spirit of adventure, with the same trepidations, and they experienced their own share of thrills along the way. In Newfoundland, where fully two-thirds of the highway was unpaved, they encountered what McCourt termed "a wide variety of terrors . . . In St. John's a big Irishman had looked at us out of eyes shrouded in a more-than-Celtic melancholy and said, 'For people like you we say special novenas.' Fifty miles out of the city we drove off paved highway onto a rock-and-gravel-surfaced trail and knew what the big Irishman meant."

Coming around a corner at high speed, the McCourts were likely to find themselves face to face with a group of children playing in the road or a herd of stray livestock, both oblivious to any danger. But they also saw some of the loveliest scenery anywhere, and Ed McCourt had to conclude that, given the difficulties the terrain presented, the miracle was that the road across The Rock existed at all.

Still vibrating from the washboard road surface, the travellers crossed by ferry to Nova Scotia where they discovered one of the drawbacks to any motorway: in the name of speed, it often reduces the countryside to a bland sameness. It was best to think of the highway as a feeder line, delivering motorists by the most direct route to the general vicinity of where they want to go, then leaving them to follow their own inclinations off the beaten path. This is particularly true of Prince Edward Island, where the Trans-Canada runs only 110 kilometres from the ferry terminal at Wood Islands through Charlottetown to Borden-Carleton, the other entrance/exit to the province.

In Hartland, New Brunswick, the McCourts crossed the town's famous covered bridge, at 391 metres the longest in the world. Officially opened in 1901, the bridge, which spans the Saint John River, is a national historic site. When it opened, tolls were charged: three cents for pedestrians, six cents for a horse and wagon, twelve cents for a double team. "Covered bridges are endowed with a quaint, old-world charm which no doubt justifies their preservation," remarked Ed McCourt, "although aesthetically they are no more pleasing than the elongated cowsheds they greatly resemble." McCourt meant his remark as a criticism, but in fact covered bridges were designed to seem familiar to animals so that horses and other livestock would not be afraid to cross them. The roof was added to protect the planks from the elements, though in winter, snow had to be shovelled into the bridges because everyone travelled by sleigh. Local tradition claims that the Hartland bridge is a "wishing bridge." When starting across, passengers in a vehicle should make a wish, cross their fingers, hold their breath and shut their eyes. If they make it across, their wish is supposed to come true.

Orwell Cove, Prince Edward Island, is in an area east of Charlottetown known for its potatoes and strawberries, as well as its Scottish festival and highland games each summer. The Trans-Canada Highway on the Island was part of Ottawa's promise to P.E.I., when the province joined Confederation in 1873, to provide transportation links with the mainland. The province's fertile red soil produces plentiful crops, but it was a handicap for highway builders, who had to import most of the rock used for construction from off the Island.

The Trans-Canada descends toward Lake Superior in Lake Superior Provincial Park in northern Ontario. This was part of the final section of highway built across central Canada.

Despite its gently undulating terrain, the Island presented its own construction problems, chief among them the need to import most of the rock used to lay the roadway's foundation. Once built, the highway hurried visitors to the capital but left them to find their own way along smaller roads to Green Gables and the north shore.

A TRAVELLER on the Trans-Canada is never far from the country's history. For much of its route the highway follows in the wake of the early explorers and traders who came from Europe in search of wealth. In New Brunswick it winds along the valley of the Saint John River where loggers once harvested the great timbers that made Maritimers the shipbuilders to the world. The broad river flows calmly past prosperous-looking farms, and white church spires stand up against the lush green hills. In its rural charm, this stretch of highway is one of the most beautiful drives in Canada. In Ontario the Trans-Canada pursues the path forged by the fur traders as they paddled up the Ottawa River and across

Lake Superior to the annual rendezvous at Fort William. Here the voyageurs celebrated another year of successful trade with a drunken blowout before they struck out westward toward the open Prairies. Across the Prairies the highway is often within sight of the Canadian Pacific main line and it does not take much imagination to picture the navvies wielding their hammers, or the colonist cars delivering immigrants from around the world to their isolated homesteads. In British Columbia, the highway follows Simon Fraser's river as it dips and plunges through the canyon he once described as a place "where no human being should venture." When he descended the river by canoe in 1808, he wrote: "I scarcely ever saw any thing so dreary, and seldom so dangerous in any country; and at present while I am writing this, whatever way I turn, mountains upon mountains, whose summits are covered with eternal snow, close the gloomy scene." Fifty years later the canyon Fraser described was flooded by tens of thousands of eager gold seekers whose presence quite literally put British

> *"Back on the highway, we watch the land curving gently, the slightest rise giving a commanding view of the land for miles around. Bales of hay dot the distant landscape. One sweep of the eye produces a farmer irrigating, a truck driving down a dirt road, somebody burning stubble, some Charolais cattle standing around. The farmhouses are set inside rings of dark green caragana trees, a typical and attractive Prairie sight."*
> Charles Gordon, *The Canada Trip*

Columbia on the map. The motorist driving the canyon today can almost hear the chink-chink of the prospector's hammer chipping away at the stoney banks in search of gold.

For travellers who are immune to the lure of history, there is always the landscape, and lots of it. Emerging from the stunted forests of northern Ontario, the driver may feel giddy as the horizon opens up to reveal what McCourt called "the terrors of infinite space".

As travellers are today, the McCourts were struck by the iconic grain elevators, the ethnic diversity of Winnipeg, the passive flatness of the Prairie landscape broken, to the south, by the low rise of the Cypress Hills, the lonely railway stations, the yellow fields of wheat. But mainly they were struck by the emptiness. "A stranger to the prairies feels uneasily that he is driving straight into infinity."

Driving through Manitoba, McCourt admitted that he and his wife had often been tempted to purchase some camping gear and give one of the many campgrounds along the highway a try. But always in the end they had resisted the temptation, preferring "the wall-to-wall broadloom" and the "posturepaedic mattresses" of motel accommodation. "There is, I think, much to be said in praise of motels," McCourt wrote, without irony. He was old enough to recall "the quaint little motels of yesteryear, each unit complete with pot-bellied stove, broken-down bed, naked overhead bulb, and privy in the bushes out back." But this did not describe the modern motels in which the McCourts lay their heads at the end of a day's driving. These were shiny new facilities, often with restaurants attached, offering the weary traveller clean rooms at affordable prices in convenient locations. Some had swimming pools and not a few even offered a black and white television set in every room. In fact, the 1960s represent the peak of the motel building boom that followed the Second World War. Subsequently the number of motels began to decline as they evolved into larger, two- and three-storey "motor lodges" and began to join corporate-owned chains such as Best Western and

Top: A motel in Ontario in 1949. Some of these places offered their customers various extras, including laundry facilities, showers, ice and so on. The earliest motels were "cottage camps" in which travellers stayed in separate cabins.

Bottom: Guests play shuffleboard at Chaffey's Lodge in Ontario in 1957. Gradually these camps gave way to the modern motel, a row of units enclosed in a single building.

Travellers who visit Ontario in late April or early May might witness the blossoming of the white trillium, the province's official flower since 1937.

Beautiful LAKE LOUISE IN THE CANADIAN ROCKIES

Banff IN THE CANADIAN ROCKIES

As they made their way through the Rocky Mountains, the McCourts were following in the wake of generations of tourists who had flocked to western Canada since the transcontinental railway was completed in 1885. To promote the use of its trains, Canadian Pacific advertised the natural wonders of the Rockies and the elegance of the CP hotels at Lake Louise and Banff.

Travelodge. In the United States in 1962, more than 98 percent of motels were operated by individual owners, whereas by 1987, 64 percent were owned by chains, and the trend was the same in Canada. In smaller communities along the Trans-Canada, where motels were less common, there was always the ubiquitous Tourist Home, a cross between the more modish Bed and Breakfast and an old-fashioned boarding house. Stephen Brook, a later cross-Canada traveller than McCourt, described these establishments as he encountered them in Newfoundland. "A Tourist Home differs from a hotel," he wrote in his book, *Maple Leaf Rag*

> in that visitors are constantly reminded that they are staying in the home of a stranger. Rules are pinned up in every room ... Tourist Homes are also guarded by fearsome landladies who always loom unexpectedly from doorways to greet you cheerily and make you feel guilty for carrying a six-pack of Labatt's up to your room (where not expressly forbidden by printed notices) and for bringing in

wetness and mud from the sodden world outside.

Most Tourist Homes are manically decorated with religious paintings, statuettes on ledges, and travel posters bright with sunshine, a visual lament for an absent friend. All the furnishings are in deep colours: green sofas are pushed back against maroon walls, and the edges of gangrenous green bedspreads lick carpets of Mediterranean blue. Beyond Calgary, the McCourts noted a significant increase in traffic as they joined the flow of travellers from the US and eastern Canada heading for the Rocky Mountains and the tourist meccas of Banff ("one of the loveliest spots on earth") and Lake Louise ("the most photographed beauty-spot on the continent.") By contrast, the Rogers Pass astonished McCourt by its seeming ordinariness, a tribute to the engineers who planned it. ("What is so great," my wife said, "about the Rogers Pass?" "What is so great about the Rogers Pass", I said, "is that we are over it.") The Pass, so impenetrable to so

Once highways were built to Yoho and Jasper national parks, the mountains were accessible to motor tourists as well. Visitors arriving at Banff by train had the option of going sightseeing on a "motor detour" in large, open touring cars like the one shown below.

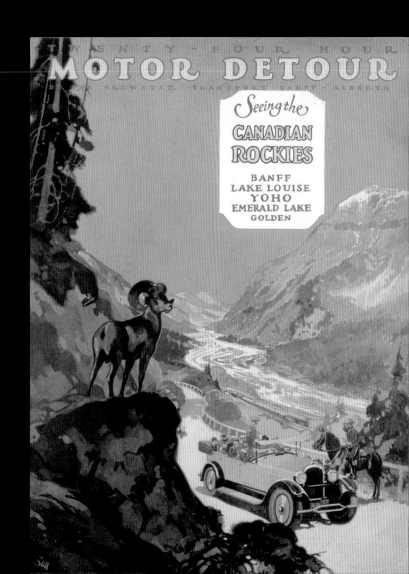

TWENTY-FOUR HOUR
MOTOR DETOUR
BY THE BREWSTER TRANSPORT, BANFF-ALBERTA

Seeing the
CANADIAN
ROCKIES

BANFF
LAKE LOUISE
YOHO
EMERALD LAKE
GOLDEN

many for so long, had become as easy to negotiate as a Sunday drive in the country.

As impressive as they found the mountains, the McCourts were self-admitted Prairie dwellers who found the interior of British Columbia a little too claustrophobic for their liking, so they hurried on to the coast. Nearly 8,000 kilometres from where they began, they came to rest at a quiet motel on the outskirts of Victoria, their journey at an end. Contemplating what they had learned from the trip, Ed McCourt concluded, paradoxically, that the country was a great deal smaller than it looked. "To travel the length of the Highway is to see Canada not as it looks on the map (a vast land of almost equal length and breadth) but as a strip of land 5,000 miles long and from 100 to 400 miles wide, compressed between one of the most populous nations on earth and a northern waste." What's more, most of this terrain consisted of "impenetrable wilderness", standing as a barrier between the few pockets of population. Even as he hoped that the new highway would be a force for national unity, the lesson that he

Newfoundland Premier Joey Smallwood (on the far side of the table, in middle) attends a banquet for the official opening of the Trans-Canada across his province in 1965. Note that the new Canadian flag, not even a year old, shares pride of place on the wall with the Union Jack, perhaps because Smallwood had opposed the new flag. "Newfoundland will continue to fly the Union Jack if we are the last people on earth to do so," he once declared.

carried away from his excursion was just how isolated the country's regions were from one another. Canadians talked about the need to develop a national identity, McCourt observed, "but no one, unless he has travelled the Trans-Canada Highway, can fully understand the degree to which our physical environment inhibits its emergence."

THE PROVINCES spent the balance of the Sixties filling in the gaps to make the Trans-Canada Highway truly trans-Canadian. The project proved to be a particular challenge for Newfoundland because the demands on its budget were so heavy. Premier Joey Smallwood and his Liberal government had discovered that after years of neglect the province required all kinds of new services: schools, hospitals, hydroelectric facilities, health and welfare programs. The Trans-Canada project necessarily took a back seat. Newfoundland had signed on to the federal-provincial agreement in 1950, but six years later, when it came time to renegotiate it, almost no progress had been made on construc-

tion. Under Robert Winters's "90/10" formula, a mere 96 kilometres of road were laid down. Finally, in 1964, with barely half the job done, Smallwood managed to use influential friends in Lester Pearson's government to extract a commitment from the federal government that it would pay for 90 percent of the remaining construction. Signs appeared beside the road announcing a new promise: We'll finish the drive in '65.

And so they did. At 11 o'clock in the morning on November 27, 1965 highways minister Eric Jones mounted an asphalt spreader and laid down the final piece of pavement. The Newfoundland section, all 980 kilometres of it, was done, and with it, so was the Trans-Canada Highway from coast to coast. Smallwood opened the new road by leading a cavalcade of cars out of St. John's. Halfway across the island, at Grand Falls, they met a similar cavalcade that had arrived from the opposite direction, led by the prime minister. The two Liberal comrades congratulated each other on a job well done, and Smallwood named a nearby hill Mount

Pearson to honour the occasion. It had taken sixteen years since Parliament passed the legislation to build the national highway. By the time the last piece of pavement dried in Newfoundland, the price tag for the nationwide route was closer to $1.4 billion ($8.8 billion in 2006 dollars) than the $300 million first estimated. Never mind, it was done.

AS CREWS LABOURED to put the finishing touches on the highway, there was a changing of the political guard in Ottawa. John Diefenbaker, who had presided over the official opening of the Trans-Canada, lost the election of 1963 to Lester Pearson and his Liberals. Instead of retiring gracefully, Diefenbaker clung to the leadership of the Conservative Party, but he grew increasingly cantankerous and irrelevant. Following another election loss in 1965, party dissidents engineered his downfall and "The Chief" was replaced in 1967 by Robert Stanfield, the bland but much-respected premier of Nova Scotia. While the Tories were going through their nasty regicide, Pearson and his Liberals were

These licence plate boosters announce Canada's centennial and the world fair, Expo 67, that was its centrepiece. Expo "is the greatest thing we have ever done as a nation," wrote journalist Peter C. Newman in the Toronto Star on the fair's opening day, April 28, 1967. The theme was "Man and His World." The graphic symbol of the fair (top left) used an ancient representation of humanity – a vertical line with outstretched arms – linked in pairs to represent friendship. Eight pairs were arranged in a circle to symbolize human brotherhood. The symbol was designed by Montreal artist Julien Hébert.

enjoying qualified acceptance from Canadian voters. For a prime minister who never managed to win a majority, Pearson's tenure in office was surprisingly crowded with achievement. The new flag, a national health insurance scheme, the Canada Pension Plan, a bilingualism policy, a unified armed forces, a royal commission on the status of women. Few minority governments have done as much, though the accomplishments tended to be overshadowed by the partisan bickering and the steady string of scandals.

The Centennial celebrations of 1967 were the crowning achievement of Lester Pearson's years in office. It was as if the public was looking for a "feel good" opportunity after years of mudslinging between Pearson and Diefenbaker that had reduced politics in Canada to a circus of insult and scandal. All across the country communities celebrated by sponsoring their own birthday projects. Dozens of local theatres, museums and parks opened. Everyone had a personal milestone to achieve. Books were written, soapbox derbys were won, mountains were scaled, beards were

grown, all to celebrate Canada. On the West coast, a real estate agent in Nanaimo named Frank Ney came up with the idea of a bathtub race across Georgia Strait to Vancouver. He presided over the event dressed as a pirate wielding a plastic sword. The citizens of St. Paul, Alberta, constructed a landing pad for flying saucers. "The only reason why UFOs have never landed in Canada," declared the secretary of the local Centennial Committee with a straight face, "is that no one has, until now, made them officially welcome." It was clearly a year for staid Canadians to let out their inner kook. The government put together a Centennial Train, painted it purple, equipped it with a steam whistle that blew *O Canada,* and launched it across the country hauling a travelling museum of history exhibits. As well, there were eight motorized "museums on wheels" that took advantage of the new national road to go wherever the railway couldn't. From the lighting of the centennial flame on Parliament Hill on January 1st to the last day in December, it was a year-long birthday bash.

Several provinces issued special licence plates to commemorate the centennial. Manitoba sold its version for five dollars and offered the chance to win a flight from Air Canada. Proceeds from the sale went toward building the Manitoba Centennial Centre. Inside the zeros, the plate features a buffalo and the centennial symbol, a stylized maple leaf. The slogan "Fun & Games" refers to the Pan-American Games, which Winnipeg hosted that summer.

Prime Minister Lester Pearson toured Expo 67 with his wife Marion (in dark glasses) and other dignitaries on the mini-rail, a small train on an elevated guideway that carried passengers around the island site.

The fair was the high-water mark of Pearson's time in office. Never had the country felt so good about itself. About 50 million visitors had passed through the gates by the time they closed for good in October.

Much of the celebration centred on the Trans-Canada Highway. It seemed as if it had been built solely to bring Canadians closer together for their birthday. To commemorate the event, people pedalled across the highway, walked across it, drove across it in vintage cars, roller-skated across it, even rode horseback across it. More conventionally, they poured down the highway in bus and car by the hundreds of thousands, from both directions, to converge on Montreal and Expo 67. Despite all the other distractions, Expo, a Class One world exhibition, was the Centennial's main event. Located on two islands in the St. Lawrence, it was a showcase of what Canada had achieved, culturally, socially, and economically. Never had the phrase "build it and they will come" had more meaning. An estimated 50 million people visited the six-month-long fair. Sixty countries built pavilions designed by some of the world's leading architects. "At Expo, we were all children," recalled Pierre Berton, "wide-eyed, titillated by the shock of the new, scampering from one outrageous pavilion to the next, our spirits lifted by the sense of gaiety, grace and good humour that these memorable structures expressed." Almost forty years later, the writer Peter C. Newman summed up the significance of the fair in his memoirs. "If Canadian nationalism was born on the killing fields of Flanders, it came of age on the pulsating grounds of the Expo world's fair. I was overwhelmed by the feeling that if this was possible, that if my frigid, self-obsessed country of twenty million people could put on this kind of spectacle, we could do almost anything . . ."

Canadians had discovered a new pride in their country, and they were determined to keep its spirit alive. No one seemed to embody this spirit more thoroughly than Justice Minister Pierre Trudeau. Trudeau had been persuaded to come to Ottawa by Lester Pearson, and when the prime minister stepped down at the end of the year, the 49-year-old former law professor from Montreal surprised everyone by winning the party leadership. (The candidate who ran a close second was none other than Robert Winters who, as minister of

Top left: Canadian hostesses at Expo 67. Each participating country had its own hostesses to show visitors around the pavilions. Countries hired their top fashion designers to come up with unique uniforms for the women.

Top right: The amusement park, known as La Ronde, was very popular with visitors, especially at night when it was transformed into a fairyland of coloured lights and fountains.

Leader of the Band

Bobby Gimby was "Canada's Pied Piper". Saskatchewan-born, he was a band leader, veteran of The Happy Gang, one of CBC-Radio's most popular shows, and a tireless writer of catchy jingles. The record of his song, the official anthem of the Centennial, sung by Gimby and a choir of children, sold more copies than any Canadian single to that time.

Canada: A Centennial Song

Ca-na-da,
(One little, two little, three Canadians)
we love thee,
(Now we are twenty million)
Ca-na-da
Proud and free.
North! South! East! West!
There'll be happy times;
Church bells will ring, ring, ring.
It's the hundreth anniversary of
Con-fed-er-ation,
Everybody sing together!

Opposite: There were many memorable sights at Expo 67, including Buckminster Fuller's geodesic dome and Moshe Safdie's multi-cellular Habitat housing project. But no person came to symbolize the fair, at least to Canadians, as much as Bobby Gimby, who wrote Expo's theme song. Dressed in a green cloak and blaring an outrageous gilded horn, Gimby was instantly recognizable that year as Canada's Pied Piper.

public works under St. Laurent, had been responsible for stick-handling the construction of the Trans-Canada.) It was the beginning of a new era.

EVEN AS THE COUNTRY basked in the warm afterglow of Expo 67, the Trans-Canada Highway still had the ability to inflame sectional feeling in some parts of the country. The federal-provincial agreement that had financed its construction lapsed in 1970. The job appeared to be accomplished. But resentment against the federal involvement in highway building lingered, most notably in British Columbia. The summer following the expiration of the agreement, Premier W.A.C. Bennett, still irritated that Ottawa did not contribute more to the maintenance of provincial highways and convinced that political power in Ottawa was controlled from Quebec, ordered the removal of all the road signs identifying the Trans-Canada Highway. At a cost of $20,000, he had them replaced with signs that said British Columbia #1. (The ill will went both ways; during this period Pierre Trudeau

referred to the B.C. premier as "the bigot who happens to run the government there".) Bennett's act of defiance lasted just a year. In August 1972, the New Democratic Party won election in British Columbia and the new government promptly reposted the Trans-Canada signs, which had been found mouldering in a warehouse where the Socreds had stashed them. Though shortlived, the episode did indicate that even if the highway was finished, the national unity it symbolized was still a long way from being achieved.

Someone once said that the automobile went from being a toy to being a luxury to being an everyday necessity, all within about thirty years. But for children, cars and trucks remain toys, to be collected, raced, traded and enjoyed. It's surprising how soon it was after the first automobiles hit the road that toy makers were manufacturing replicas for children. The racing car below dates from between 1900 and 1925. It resembles the Blitzen-Benz driven by Bob Burman when he set the Canadian speed record on July 26, 1913: one mile in 50.8 seconds, or almost 71 miles (113.5 km) an hour.

These model cars are all from the collection of the Canadian Museum of Civilization in Gatineau, Quebec.

Below are six examples: (clockwise from top left) a touring car from 1923, a milk tanker, a sporty coupe, a Ford sedan, a tow truck, and a Shell fuel truck .

Observation Peak from the Icefields
Parkway in Banff National Park, Alberta.

The Road Today

Life is a Highway
I wanna ride it all night long
If you're going my way
I wanna drive it all night long
Tom Cochrane, *Life is a Highway*

I BLAME Pierre Elliott Trudeau for introducing me to the Trans-Canada. During the 1968 federal election, "Trudeaumania" swept the country. Voters saw in the swinging bachelor from Montreal a chance to keep Canada in the spotlight that had swung in our direction during Expo 67. Trudeau dated movie stars, he drove fast sports cars, he wore sandals in the House of Commons. He was youthful and charismatic and irreverent. In the June election voters gave him the solid majority they had denied Lester Pearson for so many years.

That election was the first time I was old enough to cast a vote and was the occasion of my only in-person encounter with the soon-to-be prime minister. I was working in Vernon, British Columbia, that June when Trudeau and his entourage paid a campaign visit. The highway enters Vernon along the flank of a hillside, and down in the park where we were waiting we looked up and saw his motorcade approaching in the distance. Trudeau sat upon the back of an open convertible in a white suit, flanked by two gorgeous women, clutching what had become his trademark bouquet of

roses. Mounting the outdoor stage, he spoke for about ten minutes, rambling on about how beautiful the country was. Despite the vacuity of his remarks, the atmosphere was electric. It was as if a rock star had come to town. Change was in the air; you could feel it. The old fogies who had run Canada for so long were on the way out. I jetted down to Vancouver on election day just so that I could vote in the riding where I was registered.

It was that encounter, that amazing election campaign, that awoke in me a hankering to leave British Columbia and experience the rest of my country. Like Thomas Wilby and Jack Haney, like Percy Gomery and his "Skipper," like Dr. Doolittle and the McCourts, I wanted to drive the Trans-Canada Highway from coast to coast. When I got married three years later, my wife and I decided to relocate east, and our honeymoon became a three-month road trip. We loaded up an orange Volkswagen camper-van with our worldly possessions and set off eastward.

Being Canadians, we knew almost nothing about our country's history and

No vehicle shouts "sixties" as loudly as the Volkswagen van. The German car maker began exporting its Beetle (officially the model was called the Type 1) into Canada in 1952, and by 1960 it was selling 25,000 vehicles a year here. Volkswagen also developed the world's first minivan, the VW bus. Along with the Beetle, the van became a favourite with cost-conscious motorists who wanted a compact alternative to the chrome monsters that the major American manufacturers were producing. Despite the family focus of this 1961 brochure, the van turned out to be most popular with California surfer dudes and long-haired hippie peaceniks.

The VW Station Wagon
— the Volkswagen for Large Families
and Small Parties

had no idea that the road we were travelling was not yet a decade old. I assumed it had always been there. We poked along at a top speed of fifty-five kilometres an hour, so there was a lot of time to admire the changing landscape as it passed outside our windows. Shaped like a breadbox on wheels, the van was highly unstable in a breeze. As we wobbled over the mountains and across the Prairies, I had to grip the wheel until my fingers cramped in the face of the strong winds that tried to blow us off the road. Not long into the trip we discovered another of the van's idiosyncrasies: after a long day's driving, it refused to start the next morning. We solved this problem by always choosing campsites on a slope so that we could get underway each day with a jump-start.

I didn't truly understand how big the country was until we were leaving Winnipeg. "How long until Toronto?" my bride enquired.

"Should be there tomorrow," I replied confidently.

"I don't think so," she said, looking at the map, and of course she was right. I had not really bothered to calculate the distances, and I could see now that at our speed, Canada was several days wider than I had given it credit for.

Driving the Trans-Canada is a rite of passage, but it can also be a trial by fire. Our first night in Ontario we had barely settled into a lakeside campsite when the mosquitoes arrived. Try as we might to seal up every crack and cranny with towels and socks, the insistent insects somehow managed to make their way into the van. Swatting and cursing, we held them at bay for an hour or so. Then, seeing that sleep would be impossible, we decided to beat a retreat into our tent, where surely the zipper front would keep the bugs out. This was the first time we had used the tent on the trip, preferring the comforts of the van at night, so we were surprised to find that I had forgotten to pack the poles. Never mind; we were desperate. Raising the roof of the tent by tying it to the van's rearview mirror, we managed to clamber inside just as a heavy rain began falling. The tent was not waterproof. Back inside the van we went, taking our

It was like having a rock star for a prime minister. Everywhere he went, Pierre Trudeau was besieged by fans demanding his autograph. Expo 67 ushered in a new era for Canada, and Trudeau seemed to personify the youthful, self-confident spirit that had infected the country. Completely unknown outside Quebec when he was elected to Parliament in 1965, three years later he was prime minister and Canadians were breaking down doors to get close to him.

Magnetic Hill near Moncton, N.B.--18.

"Wish you were here . . ." As this old hand-tinted postcard shows, Magnetic Hill outside Moncton, New Brunswick, has been attracting Trans-Canada motorists for many years. The idea is to park at the bottom of the hill; the parked vehicle is then drawn backwards up the slope by a "mysterious" force.

cushions with us, and spent the dark hours hammering the metal sides of the vehicle with rolled-up magazines in a vain attempt to kill off the last mosquito. But the bugs kept coming, like an invincible army. By this time we were laughing hysterically; one can only wonder what travellers in the neighbouring campsites thought was going on. Finally, we fell asleep from exhaustion. When we rose the next morning, my wife counted fifty-one bites on my back alone. We pulled away from the campsite wondering what other delights of nature Ontario had in store for us. (It seems only fitting that down the road at Upsala, Ontario, a giant steel and fibreglass mosquito has been erected beside the highway, carrying away a life-sized replica of a man, in homage to the local pest.)

When we left Vancouver our destination had been Ottawa, where I had been more or less promised a job. But when we arrived the promise was broken, so we decided to continue our trip down the Trans-Canada all the way to Halifax to see what life there might offer. The

drive down the Saint John River Valley is still, for my money, the most beautiful length of highway in the country. While we feasted on the scenery, we read an Agatha Christie mystery out loud to each other. Like legions of tourists before us, we visited Magnetic Hill near Moncton, pondered the reversing falls at Saint John and crossed to Prince Edward Island to eat lobster and visit Anne Shirley's house. A trip along the highway is full of iconic moments: hearing a loon on a rippled lake, passing through the majesty of the Rocky Mountains, watching a weathered grain elevator grow large on the horizon, catching first sight of the Parliament Buildings in Ottawa. Our crossing from New Brunswick into Nova Scotia was another of these. At the exact moment that the "Welcome to Nova Scotia" sign loomed up ahead of us, "Squid Jigging Ground" began playing on the radio. We took this as an omen that Halifax held good things for us. We were wrong.

Subsequently I have visited Halifax many times and have come to admire it, but that first encounter was like a bad

This is one of the earliest guidebooks on the completed highway, published in 1967, the centennial year. It is a collection of detailed maps and descriptions of the sights travellers should expect to see along the route.

Contrary to the book's cover, the Trans-Canada has never been Highway 1 everywhere across the country. Because it absorbed many already completed roads, it goes by several different numbers. For example, in northern Ontario it is 17; on the south shore of the St. Lawrence it is 20; through New Brunswick it is 2; and in Nova Scotia it is 104. But in the hearts and minds of Canadian drivers, it is the number one highway across the country.

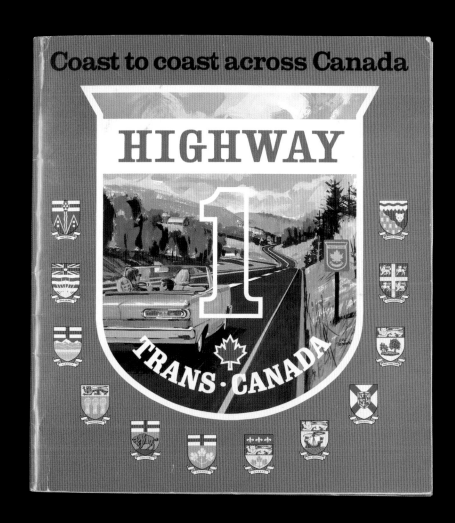

Coast to coast across Canada

HIGHWAY 1

TRANS·CANADA

The placid waters of the Saint John River near Woodstock, New Brunswick.

The hamlet of Capstick on the coast of Cape Breton Island, Nova Scotia, not far from where the author and his bride ended their cross-Canada drive.

first date. The weather was foul, the streets were empty and the newspapers, where I intended to seek a job, were inferior.

But we refused to be discouraged. In the spirit of the open road, we were footloose and ready for anything, and we still had a few dollars left in the bank account. We simply repacked the van and moved on. We decided to drive to the farthest point east on the continental mainland, which as far as we could tell from the map was a little hamlet called Meat Cove hanging off the northern tip of Cape Breton. We found it at the end of a dirt road and stood gazing out at the Atlantic, pleased with ourselves at having gone coast to coast. Mission accomplished – Newfoundland would have to wait for another trip – we got back on the Trans-Canada and returned to Ottawa to settle down and earn a living like responsible adults.

THE TRANS-CANADA has been the setting for many personal adventures like ours, but at times it has also been a stage on which our most compelling national dramas have been acted out. In the sum-

mer of 1980, motorists barrelling down the highway came across a strange cavalcade: a solitary runner, his shorts revealing an artificial leg, running westward along the road, accompanied by a camper-van emblazoned with "MARATHON OF HOPE CROSS COUNTRY RUN IN AID OF CANCER RESEARCH." Many drivers didn't know who he was or what he was doing, but Terry Fox was on his way to becoming a Canadian legend. Three years earlier, as an eighteen-year-old student athlete, Fox had learned he had bone cancer in his right leg. Doctors amputated above the knee and fitted him with a prosthesis. Fox didn't let his artificial leg slow him down. He played wheelchair basketball, took up running and in the fall of 1979 came up with a plan to raise money to fight the disease that had taken his leg. He would stage his Marathon of Hope, running across Canada to ask people to donate to the cause.

Of all the expeditions that had crossed the Trans-Canada, Fox's was the most inspiring. On April 12, 1980, he began at St. John's in the traditional manner,

The Trans-Canada had never seen such compelling drama as Terry Fox's Marathon of Hope. He left St. John's, Newfoundland, on April 12, 1980, intending to follow the highway all the way to the other side of the country. When he started out, hardly anyone knew about his campaign to raise money for cancer research. By the time he was forced to leave the highway near Thunder Bay, Ontario, Canadians were riveted by his courage.

"I loved it. I enjoyed myself so much, and that was what other people couldn't realize. They thought I was going through a nightmare running all day long. People thought I was going through hell. Maybe I was, partly, but still I was doing what I wanted and a dream was coming true, and that, above everything else, made it all worthwhile to me. Even though it was so difficult, there was not another thing in the world I would rather have been doing."

Terry Fox

dipping his leg into the ice-cold Atlantic before setting out. The mayor of the city, Dorothy Wyatt, ran with him, dressed in a polka-dot pantsuit and her chain of office. Momentum grew slowly. At first it was a solitary business, just Fox and a school friend who drove the van, out on the road by dawn every morning no matter what the weather, plodding along through ice, lightning storms, heavy rain, fierce headwinds and intense heat. By the time he reached Ontario the public had cottoned on to what the runner was doing. He acquired a police escort, and people lined the road, welcoming him with brass bands and tearful applause as he passed through their towns. Other runners joined him on the road, including his younger brother, Darrell. In Ottawa he made a ceremonial kickoff at a CFL game and met Prime Minister Trudeau. In Toronto a crowd of ten thousand well-wishers packed Nathan Phillips Square to honour the one-legged crusader, raising a one-day total of $100,000. Fox celebrated his twenty-second birthday on the road in Gravenhurst, north of Toronto, by

which time the entire country was watching the marathon and cheering him on.

By August 12 Fox had reached Sudbury and had raised $1.4 million, but his strength was beginning to flag. He had been running the equivalent of a marathon a day (42.2 kilometres) for four months on one leg. He kept on going, but on September 1, approximately 12 kilometres before Thunder Bay, after 143 days on the road, his body racked with pain, he had to stop. Doctors at a local hospital conveyed the sad news that the cancer had spread to his lungs. The next day Fox told a news conference that he would have to abandon the run after 5,373 kilometres and return home to British Columbia. He promised to return to the highway and continue the run.

As Fox underwent treatment, the money and the honours poured in. He became the youngest person awarded a Companion of the Order of Canada and was named Canadian of the Year by a panel of newspaper editors. But the cancer continued to spread, finally claiming his life on June 28, 1981. Within three

months the first Terry Fox Run took place to honour his memory. More than three hundred thousand people participated around the world, raising $3.2 million for cancer research. The run has since become an annual September rite and has raised hundreds of millions of dollars.

Shortly after Fox's death, an eighty-three-kilometre stretch of the Trans-Canada Highway between Thunder Bay and Nipigon, Ontario, was named the Terry Fox Courage Highway. On June 26, 1982, dignitaries dedicated a monument to the young runner at Terry Fox Lookout, beside the highway just west of where he was forced to abandon his Marathon of Hope. The monument includes a 2.7-metre-tall bronze statue of Fox, made by the Ontario sculptor Manfred of Oakville. The statue is mounted on a granite base that depicts the coats of arms of all the provinces and territories, along with emblems of the beaver and the maple leaf, Canada's two iconic symbols.

Steve Fonyo is the other one-legged runner, the one who is forgotten, the one who actually made it. Fonyo was a

Fox trained for his Marathon of Hope for more than two years. In 1979, in Prince George, B.C., he ran his first long-distance race. He crossed the finish line in last place, but the experience convinced him that his dream of running across Canada was a possibility. He kept a meticulous record of his training routine in a pocket diary. Below, the diary's final page notes his departure for St. John's in April 1980. He had run a total of 5,055 kilometres to get himself ready. Fox was accompanied on the marathon by his school friend, Doug Alward, who drove the van that they camped in when there was no motel around.

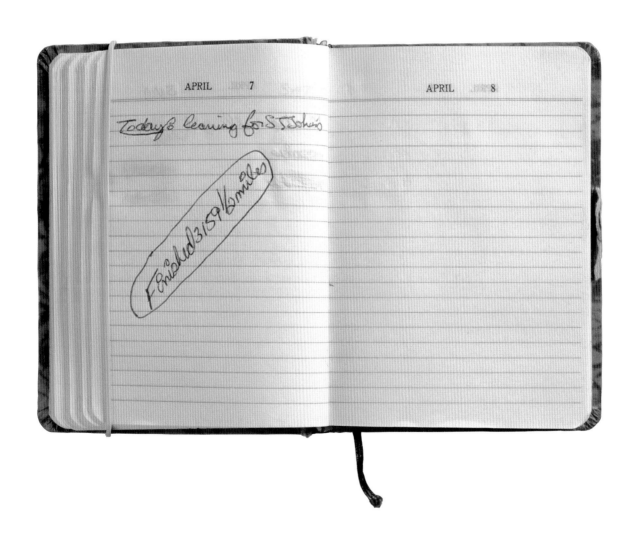

East meets west. Suzanne Krupa helps her brother, Steve Fonyo, empty into the Pacific Ocean a jar of water he brought from the Atlantic. Fonyo's run across Canada, overshadowed by Terry Fox's earlier attempt, raised more than $13 million for cancer research. The spot where he ended his run in Victoria is now known as Steve Fonyo Beach. Fonyo was named to the Order of Canada in 1987.

twelve-year-old kid when he lost his left leg to bone cancer. Three years later, along with the rest of the country, he watched Terry Fox attempt his Marathon of Hope. When Fox was forced to abandon his run, Fonyo decided to pick up the challeng and make a run of his own. His Journey for Lives marathon began in St. John's on March 31, 1984. At first he loped along the highway in near anonymity, but once he passed Thunder Bay and the spot where Fox had to give up, Fonyo came out from under the shadow of the other runner and began to receive the attention the press and public had been withholding. The Journey for Lives lasted fourteen months. By the time Fonyo reached the end of the highway in Victoria, his effort had raised more than $13 million for cancer research.

PROBABLY THE MOST HEROIC test of endurance to involve the Trans-Canada Highway was the Man In Motion World Tour, launched by a Vancouver paraplegic athlete named Rick Hansen. Shortly after Terry Fox had been diagnosed with cancer, Hansen had recruited him for a wheelchair basketball team and the two became good friends. Hansen, who had lost the use of his legs in a road accident when he was fifteen, was studying physical education at the University of British Columbia. He had been considering taking on the challenge of a long-distance wheelchair campaign to raise awareness, and money, for spinal cord research, and it was Fox's example that motivated him to put his thoughts into action. On March 21, 1985, Hansen, the self-dubbed "Man In Motion," left Vancouver to begin a monumental journey during which he would wheel himself through thirty-four countries on four continents in twenty-six months. His world tour took him across the United States, through Great Britain and much of western Europe, down the Arabian Peninsula, through parts of Australia and New Zealand, even along the Great Wall of China.

The final leg of the tour brought Hansen back to Canada where in August 1986 he started out on the Trans-Canada Highway at St. John's, heading for British Columbia and home. To that point,

Rick Hansen wheels his way through some foul winter weather in the interior of British Columbia in March 1987, near the end of his Man In Motion World Tour.

During the tour, which covered forty thousand kilometres, Hansen spent 792 days on the road, and wore out 160 wheelchair tires and 94 pairs of gloves.

Dangerous driving conditions are a fact of life on the Trans-Canada in winter, even in the country's most temperate province. Here, vehicles have been abandoned after skidding off the highway between Abbotsford and Chilliwack in B.C.'s Fraser Valley during a sudden snowstorm in March 2002. A tow truck driver is retrieving a smashed car part from the divided highway.

while the tour had been a remarkable story of achievement, it had raised less than two percent of its fundraising target of $10 million. It was in Canada, where the Man In Motion was hailed as a returning hero, that people opened their hearts, and their wallets. The generosity began immediately in Newfoundland, where in two days the tour collected close to $100,000; escalated through Ottawa, where Prime Minister Brian Mulroney handed over a cheque for $1 million from the federal government; and rolled on across the country. And it was not just the money, though the tour topped out at $26 million. Hansen considered himself an ambassador for the disabled. "We were trying to provide an illustration that all disabled persons must struggle every day in pursuit of a normal life," he later wrote, "and that, as with the tour, amazing things can happen once those obstacles are removed." Everywhere he went he spoke about the need to lower the barriers, both physical and psychological, that kept people with disabilities from achieving their potential.

The Trans-Canada in winter is a tough slog for motorists inside their heated cars, let alone for a man in a wheelchair exposed to ice and sleet, battling headwinds sweeping down from the Arctic. But Hansen struggled on, the end now in sight. He crossed the Prairies in the subzero temperatures of deep winter, traversed the Rockies, wheeled up and over Rogers Pass and finally, on May 22, 1987, rolled into the parking lot in Vancouver where it had all begun. The final tally was forty thousand kilometres and more than twice the amount of money raised than the target Hansen had set himself.

THE ACCOMPLISHMENTS of Terry Fox, Steve Fonyo and Rick Hansen make it clear that the Trans-Canada has come to be more than just another road. When Canadians want to draw attention to a cause or accomplish something together as a nation, they seem irresistibly drawn to the highway. Along with some amazing feats of endurance, this tendency has brought about some audacious feats of construction. The mountain passes and

the section of highway north of Superior are two examples. Another is the Confederation Bridge.

According to the terms under which Prince Edward Island joined Canada in 1873, the federal government promised to maintain a year-round connection between the Island and the mainland. This promise was easier to make than to keep. P.E.I. is separated from Nova Scotia and New Brunswick by the Northumberland Strait, which is up to seventeen kilometres wide and is choked by ice for several months of the year. In the early years it was not always possible to keep connections open, and the federal commitment was a leitmotif running through relations between the province and the central government. Paddlewheel steamers were used in the summer months, but these were inoperable in the ice and were supplemented by iceboats during the winter. For twelve years a government steamer called the Northern Light plied the strait. Since the stern of this wooden vessel turned out to be stronger than the bow for breaking through ice, it often

Highways Over Water

The new Confederation Bridge meant the end of one ferry service on the Trans-Canada system, but three other vital marine links remain.

Travellers to Prince Edward Island can still opt to take the car ferry that travels back and forth across the Northumberland Strait between Wood Islands and Caribou, Nova Scotia. Farther east, motorists embark on the ferry to Newfoundland at North Sydney on Cape Breton Island. There has been a ferry to Port aux Basques since the *SS Bruce* went into service in 1898. There was no road across Newfoundland, of course, but a railway had been built during the 1890s. In 1925 the *SS Caribou* took over the route and plied the Cabot Strait for seventeen years, until the night of October 14, 1942. The war was raging in Europe and German U-boats were known to be patrolling the entrance to the Gulf of St. Lawrence. The *Caribou* left

North Sydney for its regular run with 237 passengers and crew on board. It was accompanied by a naval escort, but that made no difference. A German torpedo found the ferry amidships and down it went, taking 137 people with it. The Halifax Herald called the incident the greatest marine disaster of the war in Canadian waters. Visitors to Newfoundland will find a monument to the tragedy in a park at Port aux Basques. They will also find themselves making the

ferry crossing on the *MV Caribou*, a modern, high-speed version of the original.

At the other end of the country, a ferry service transports vehicles between mainland British Columbia and Vancouver Island. BC Ferries was another idea from the fertile brain of Premier W.A.C. Bennett. In 1958 a labour dispute disrupted the privately owned ferry service at the time. Bennett seized on the opportunity to announce that his government was going into

the business. "Bennett's Navy," as the publicly owned British Columbia Ferry Authority was known, launched its first vessels in June 1960. A year later it bought the Black Ball Line and took over the run between Horseshoe Bay and Nanaimo, the route that now forms part of the Trans-Canada. BC Ferries, which was privatized in 2003, now operates about forty vessels on more than two dozen routes, making it one of the world's largest ferry systems.

Top: At its highest point the Confederation Bridge is 60 metres above the waters of the strait, allowing large vessels to pass underneath. The roadway, where the speed limit is 80 kilometres an hour, is curved in an attempt to keep drivers more attentive. Vehicles are not allowed to stop or to pass. The piers had to be specially designed so that ice would not pile up against them in the winter and overwhelm the bridge.

Opposite: Wind and ice make the Northumberland Strait a treacherous place for a bridge. Skeptics doubted it was feasible, but engineers proved them wrong. The bridge was built using the world's largest floating crane, three times taller than P.E.I.'s tallest building.

made the winter crossing backwards. On at least one occasion passengers had to abandon the iced-in vessel and make their way to land on foot across the floes. Construction of more effective icebreakers improved the situation, but some Islanders began to lobby for a fixed link in the form of a tunnel under the strait. In 1917 a steam-powered railcar ferry began service, linking P.E.I. to New Brunswick and the transcontinental railway system. This vessel provided the first reliable all-weather crossings; iceboats were finally a thing of the past. Still, it was the 1930s before the popularity of automobile travel convinced the government to add a car deck to its ferry. By the post-war period, travellers had a choice of two ferry services to the Island, one from New Brunswick and the other from Nova Scotia.

The idea of a fixed link continued to percolate, but in the form of a causeway instead of a tunnel. During the 1960s federal governments under both the Conservatives and the Liberals promised a causeway, and at one point, in 1965, sod was even turned to mark the begin-

ning of construction. But that was as far as the project got. It was abandoned during one of Ottawa's periodic austerity campaigns, and when talk of a fixed link resurfaced, a bridge had become the preferred option. In 1987 the federal government asked for expressions of interest from companies wanting to build a link, a move that brought simmering opposition to the project to a boil. Critics of the idea worried that a bridge would harm the local fishery and that the unique Island lifestyle would be overrun by tourists. The debate was intense, culminating in a 1988 plebiscite in which fifty-nine percent of Islanders voted in favour of a link. Subsequently a private consortium, Strait Crossing Inc., won the contract and built the bridge between Cape Jourimain N.W.A., New Brunswick, and Borden-Carleton, P.E.I., at a cost of $1 billion.

The two-lane Confederation Bridge (the name was chosen from suggestions submitted by the public) opened to traffic on May 31, 1997. At 12.9 kilometres, it's the longest bridge in the world over ice-covered water. It is a toll bridge, the

The text on the sign reads:

UNDER THE AUTHORITY
of
PARLIAMENT
The Gore and Vaughan Plank Road
rate of Tolls to be collected thereon
for each time passing whether loaded
or otherwise
for every Vehicle drawn by two Horses
or other Cattle   £ . s . D 6
for every additional horse or beast   0 . 0 . 2
   "   "   Vehicle drawn by one horse 0 . 0 . 3
   "   "   Horse Ass or Mule   0 . 0 . 2
   "   "   score of Neat Cattle   0 . 0 . 1
   "   "   score of Sheep or Swine   0 . 0 . 1
                    By order of the Directors
Dated Jan. 1st 1851

Tolls date back to Canada's pioneer days, when roads were built by private companies that were allowed to charge fees for using them. The practice began with wagons and livestock and later was extended to automobiles. Tolls varied, of course, depending on the kind of vehicle, the number of animals and the quality of the road. Owners of this plank road in Ontario in 1851 charged sixpence for a wagon and two horses. Tolls are not a thing of the past. The Confederation Bridge charges motorists to cross, and there are tolls on sections of the Trans-Canada in New Brunswick and Nova Scotia. Increasingly, provincial politicians look to tolls as a way of financing much-needed improvements to the highway system.

only one on the Trans-Canada; in 2005 motorists paid $39.50 to make the ten-minute drive across. While the bridge did not transform Prince Edward Island into a Coney Island-like amusement park, as some people feared, it did contribute to a fifty percent jump in visitors during the first year of its operation.

IN THE BOOK HE WROTE about his drive across the country in 1963, Ed McCourt waxed nostalgic for "the almost-forgotten time when each car was a distinct personality – perverse, idiosyncratic, lovable, and hateful, like a dog or horse obedient only to the master familiar with its ways, and responsive to persuasions (including the occasional well-placed kick) unknown to the modern mechanic." For most of us, that time is long gone, as it was for McCourt. But in 1997 two history buffs set out to revisit the days when an automobile was still called a "horseless carriage."

Remember Thomas Wilby and Jack Haney, the mismatched pair who drove across Canada (sort of) in 1912? Eighty-five years later to the day (August 27),

In Manitoba, west of Winnipeg, fields of canola stretch away to the horizon. It was not until after the Second World War that canola became popular with western farmers, so Wilby and Haney would not have seen any of the bright yellow flowers.

Lorne Findlay stands beside his vintage Reo. In 1997, along with writer John Nicol, Findlay and his Reo managed to replicate the famous drive across Canada made eighty-five years earlier by Jack Haney and Thomas Wilby.

another pair of automaniacs set off from Halifax driving a vintage Reo to recreate the original trip. At the wheel was Lorne Findlay, a seventy-year-old antique car buff from British Columbia. In the passenger seat, playing the role of Thomas Wilby, was John Nicol, a writer from Ontario. The Reo, which Findlay had acquired in 1980, was the same make, model and year as the original. The plan was to stop in the same places on the same days as the original travellers. As concessions to modernity, the replicators were supported by a second vehicle and a website, along with the ghosts of Wilby and Haney riding in the back seat.

Sometimes Findlay and Nicol were able to stay in the very same hotels as their predecessors, but more often than not, these establishments had fallen victim to fire or been turned into strip clubs, a visible reminder of how much had changed in eighty-five years. Many of the things the modern-day travellers saw through the window of the Reo remained unchanged: the parish churches in the small villages beside the St. Lawrence, the vast distances of rock and tree north of Lake Superior,

the fields of standing grain in the Prairies, the breathtaking majesty of the Rocky Mountains. There was something charmingly convivial about the expedition. At every town along the route, Findlay and Nicol were greeted by members of the local vintage car club, and the Reo turned out to be a magnet for an engaging array of auto enthusiasts who welcomed the chance to swap stories. There was the blind mechanic in Halifax who had lost his sight as a child in the great explosion of 1917 yet worked with cars all his life. There was the Quebec senior, Phil Latulippe, who had run across Canada three times for charity, the last time when he was seventy years old. There were the two old-timers who had worked on relief, building the highway west of Thunder Bay in the 1930s, and the guy in Alberta who used to race souped-up Model Ts. Some of these senior citizens were even older than the Reo, whose presence seemed to prompt an outpouring of nostalgia.

The modern travellers found the road a good deal more civilized than it had been in 1912. There were gas stations,

convenience stores, shopping malls, restaurants and comfortable motels. Scenic viewpoints were denoted with tidy plaques, and road crews filled in the potholes. Thanks to Lorne Findlay's mechanical know-how, the Reo performed like a charm. Problems were confined to the engine overheating on occasion and the odd spark plug needing replacement. "We had more problems with computers and phones along the way than we had with the Reo," observed Nicol in the book he wrote about the excursion. This was a far cry from the original expedition, which was forever getting bogged down in swamps or running out of road in the middle of nowhere.

After fifty-three days on the road, Findlay and Nicol sped into Victoria, accompanied by the now-familiar caravan of local antique cars, and drew up in front of the provincial legislature for a small ceremony to celebrate the completion of their 8,228-kilometre drive. In 1912 Wilby and Haney had been feted at the Pacific Club that evening with a dinner that featured oysters, roast beef, litres of champagne

Mac the Moose receives a fresh coat of paint. At ten metres high, Mac is advertised as "the world's largest moose." Certainly he is the largest moose that travellers along the Trans-Canada will ever catch sight of. All nine thousand kilograms of him stands at the visitor information centre in Moose Jaw, Saskatchewan.

At the Side of the Road

Given that the Trans-Canada is the longest national highway in the world, it's fitting that it harbours some of the largest, and strangest, roadside attractions ever conceived.

The Wawa goose and the giant mosquito are just the tip of the iceberg. The road begins in Victoria within sight of the world's tallest totem pole carved from a single tree. By the time motorists have reached the ferry terminal in Nanaimo, they have already encountered the world's largest bathtub (to com-memorate the annual bathtub race across the strait to Vancouver) and the world's largest hockey stick and puck. The Fraser Canyon offers a giant rocking chair, Kamloops a giant trout, Revelstoke a very large Smokey the Bear.

British Columbia merely sets the pattern. All across the country communities have vied for the traveller's attention by installing outsized monuments beside the highway. Medicine Hat has a sixty-five-metre-tall teepee originally built for the 1988 Calgary Winter Olympics. Moose Jaw has a ten-metre-high moose, named Mac after a one-time city alderman. For fishing enthusiasts, Kenora offers Husky the Musky, a two and-a-half tonne replica of a fish, while Sudbury has become famous for the Big Nickel. There are enough animals – deer, geese, buffaloes, gophers, bears, turtles and, of course, beavers – to fill Noah's Ark. There is even fruit: a giant straw-berry at Deer Lake, Newfoundland, and an eight-tonne steel blueberry outside Oxford, Nova Scotia, the self-declared blueberry capital of the world.

At Strathclair Park in Sault Ste. Marie, a huge baseball lies in the grass as if left behind by a team of giants.

In Echo Bay, Ontario, east of the Sault, the "Big Loo-nie", not to be confused with Sudbury's Big Nickel, was designed by a local resident in 1987.

Signal Hill, overlooking the harbour of St. John's, Newfoundland, is one of the Trans-Canada's two mile zeros. Here the Italian inventor Guglielmo Marconi received the world's first transatlantic radio transmission, sent in Morse code from Cornwall, England, on December 12, 1901. The castle-like Cabot Tower was completed in 1900 to commemorate the four hundredth anniversary of John Cabot's voyage to Newfoundland.

and Wilby's stock speech in support of a national highway. The modern travellers opted instead to catch a ferry back to the mainland, eager to return to the comforts of home.

PRIME MINISTER William Lyon Mackenzie King once remarked that Canada had too much geography and not enough history, but a trip across Canada's national road, whether by vintage car, camper-van or family sedan, is an excursion into both.

At Field, British Columbia, for example, the driver passes the world-famous Burgess Shale, where fossil finds date back 530 million years. The shale has been named a World Heritage Site by the United Nations. So has Dinosaur Provincial Park, just a short drive off the highway in the heart of Alberta's badlands, where dinosaurs once made their home. On a more human scale, the historic district of Quebec City, with its narrow cobblestoned streets, has also earned World Heritage status. The highway passes through five national parks, from the rocky headlands of Terra Nova on the east coast of

Newfoundland to the epic grandeur of the mountain parks of British Columbia. At one end of the country, the road begins at a historic site, Signal Hill, overlooking St. John's harbour where in 1901 Guglielmo Marconi received the world's first transoceanic radio message. At the other end it originates in Victoria's Beacon Hill Park, not far from the Empress Hotel, one of Canadian Pacific's distinctive chateau-style railway hotels. In between, the highway deposits the traveller at dozens of historic sites, from the Alexander Graham Bell museum in Baddeck, Nova Scotia, to the Plains of Abraham in Quebec, from the reconstructed fur-trading post of Fort William in Thunder Bay to the RCMP museum in Regina to the forest of poles in the City of Totems in Duncan, B.C. Driving the Trans-Canada is like taking a crash course in Canadian history and geography.

The Trans-Canada Highway makes up thirty percent of the country's much larger National Highway System (NHS), a 24,459-kilometre road system that includes all primary highways linking

Dinosaur Provincial Park is just off the Trans-Canada in southeastern Alberta. Vegetation there is sparse, and the soft sandstone has been shaped by the elements into an exotic lunar landscape. The park is a UNESCO World Heritage Site because of its plentiful fossil remains.

major population centres and border crossings. This extensive network of paved highways, though it accounts for just three percent of Canada's total roads, carries a quarter of all motor vehicle traffic in the country. The Trans-Canada itself has expanded from the original single route across the country to include a variety of alternative routes. Between Nova Scotia and New Brunswick, for example, motorists can stick to the mainland or follow the route across the Northumberland Strait through Prince Edward Island. There are two routes west of Montreal into Ontario and several routes through Ontario. Out west, the original highway follows the same route as the Canadian Pacific Railway, from Winnipeg to Regina, Calgary, Banff and the Kicking Horse Pass through the Rockies. In 1970 an alternative northern route dubbed the Yellowhead Highway opened. It diverges from the main highway at Portage la Prairie, Manitoba; angles in a northwesterly direction through Saskatoon and Edmonton; crosses the Rockies via Jasper and the Yellowhead Pass; and continues

across British Columbia to reach the Pacific at Prince Rupert.

Since the Trans-Canada opened in 1962, work on improving it has not ceased. Much like the country it traverses, the highway is a work in progress. Interchanges are improved, sections are repaved and "twinned" (a second lane added in each direction), passing lanes are created. In the mountain parks the increased incidence of deadly encounters between motor vehicles and wildlife has led to the construction of unique four-legged pedestrian crossings, both overpasses and underpasses, that allow elk, moose, bear and other park animals to get to the other side without endangering life and limb. Nevertheless, as traffic volumes have increased and vehicles have become larger and faster, improvements have not kept pace with the rate at which the National Highway System is deteriorating.

In 1988 officials from the provincial and federal governments agreed to launch a study to assess the state of Canadian highways. This study found that thirty-eight percent of the NHS did not measure

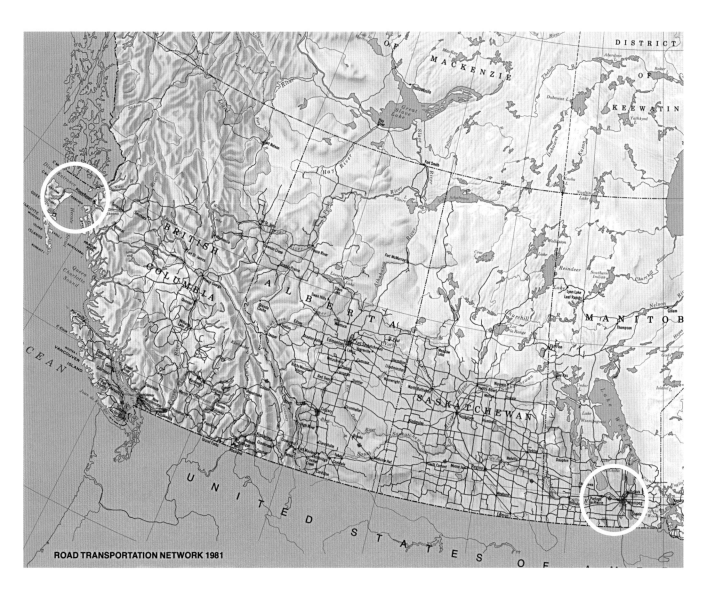

ROAD TRANSPORTATION NETWORK 1981

This map shows the route of the Yellowhead Highway, part of an expanded Trans-Canada system. The Yellowhead crosses the middle of the prairies from Portage la Prairie, Manitoba, to Edmonton, Alberta; leaps the Rocky Mountains through the Yellowhead Pass; then continues to the coast via Prince George and the Skeena River Valley. At Prince Rupert the highway is extended by ferry across Hecate Strait to the Queen Charlotte Islands (Haida Gwaii). Designated Highway 16 for its entire length, the Yellowhead route was officially incorporated into the Trans-Canada system in 1986.

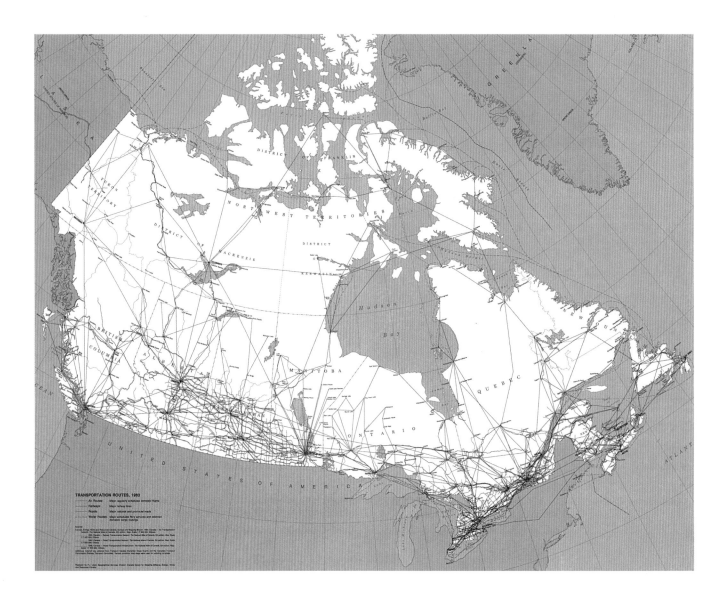

TRANSPORTATION ROUTES, 1983

This map from the Atlas of Canada shows major transportation routes – air, rail, road and water – in 1983. In the 1980s officials began to be aware that Canadian highways were deteriorating at an alarming rate. According to a study launched in 1988, more than a third of the National Highway System, which consists of the Trans-Canada and other primary highways, did not meet basic standards of design and repair. Experts agree that since that time the situation has gotten worse, not better.

The Trans-Canada has provided a platform for many protests over the years. Here, trucker Jason Harper joins a North America–wide outcry against skyrocketing fuel prices on September 6, 2005. Hundreds of big rigs stopped along the highway at weigh scales and truck stops to draw attention to the strain high prices were putting on their livelihood.

up to minimum standards. Almost 800 of the 3,534 bridges that are part of the NHS needed strengthening or repair. The estimate was $12.7 billion to get the system up to minimum standards. As of 1989 forty percent of the Trans-Canada was already four lanes wide or better. The study said it would cost another $5 billion to complete the job, creating a continuous four-lane highway across Canada. If this work was done, the study estimated that the resulting highway improvements would save 160 lives a year, not to mention the various economic gains that come from faster, safer highways. Of course, highways are not simply an expenditure for government. The federal government alone takes in about $4 billion a year in fuel taxes, while the provinces earn several billion more from taxes, licence fees, vehicle registration and other fees. Promoters of better roads point out that only a fraction of this revenue is invested back into highways.

A further review of the situation in 1997 discovered that despite increased expenditures on the highway system, even more of it was below minimum standards than ten years earlier, and the cost of correcting the situation had climbed to $17.4 billion. In November 2000 a tour bus carrying twenty-four Taiwanese tourists collided with a truck east of Revelstoke in the Rogers Pass area of British Columbia, killing five people including the bus driver. This horrible accident spotlighted just how treacherous some parts of the highway still were and left many Canadians wondering if the Trans-Canada had become a death trap.

In 2001 the federal government announced the Strategic Highway Infrastructure Program. SHIP was a five-year, $600 million program to upgrade the nation's main highways. As part of this program, major projects were undertaken all along the Trans-Canada. In British Columbia upgrades began on the narrow, twisting road through the Kicking Horse Canyon near Golden, built in the 1950s and unimproved since then. Between 1996 and 2001 there were seven hundred accidents along this stretch of highway, claiming twenty-one lives. In Saskatchewan the twinning of the Trans-Canada right

The post office issued this five-cent highway safety stamp on May 2, 1966, to coincide with the Canadian Highway Safety Council's annual conference in Calgary. Council members were concerned that traffic accidents were killing, injuring or causing property damage at a pace of one mishap every one and a half minutes. Every two hours someone died on the road. In response to these statistics, the council lobbied for mandatory seatbelt use. The battle for safer roads continues today. Activists seeking improvements to the Trans-Canada claim that hundreds of lives could be saved annually if the highway were brought up to modern standards.

across the province was scheduled to be finished by 2007. Likewise, in Quebec the highway was twinned south from Rivière-du-Loup to the New Brunswick border, while twinning of the 516 kilometres through New Brunswick will be completed by 2007.

In essence, as the new millennium began, governments joined together just as they had in 1949 to rebuild the Trans-Canada to modern standards. However, just as they had in 1949, the provinces and Ottawa could not always agree on who was responsible for doing what, and how much was enough. According to highway lobby groups such as the Canadian Automobile Association and the Canadian Trucking Alliance, SHIP was a drop in the bucket. They said that billions of dollars more would be required to make the Trans-Canada an efficient, safe highway.

Anyone driving the road in the summer of 2005 would have had no trouble picking out its deficiencies: red lights that interrupt the flow of traffic; too many kilometres of two-lane road; harrowing sections where motorists are hung up behind, or between, giant logging trucks or long-distance haulers; routes that carry vehicles through major cities instead of around them; poorly designed exits and entrances. Jeffrey Simpson, national affairs columnist for *The Globe and Mail*, summed it up after driving from Alberta to Ontario: "Nowhere . . . does the Trans-Canada remotely resemble a U.S. interstate, a German autobahn, a French autoroute, an Italian autostrada or a British motorway. Instead, it looks much more like what people in those countries would call a secondary road . . . It's a highway for handling modest but not large amounts of traffic, and certainly not an essential engine of commerce for a modern economy." This is the challenge facing the engineers and the policy makers – how to make today's deteriorating Trans-Canada a modern highway for tomorrow.

LONG BEFORE ITS COMPLETION, the Trans-Canada Highway was envisioned as an important force for national unity. In his book about his cross-Canada jaunt in 1912, Thomas Wilby stated the case:

Pedestrians walk across the twin bridges spanning the Saint John River east of Fredericton, New Brunswick, on October 23, 2001, the day before the bridges officially opened to vehicle traffic as part of an upgrade of this section of the Trans-Canada. Twinning of the highway across New Brunswick is expected to be complete by 2007. The creation of a four-lane Trans-Canada right across the country is the ultimate objective of highway planners.

**Cars on the Trans-Canada
at dusk, on the Mile Hill
north of Sault Ste. Marie.**

"It was the dream of Sir James Douglas and is still the hope of all Canadians to whom national unity is a passionately desired end that a Trans-Canada highway should draw closer together all parts of the nation and help us, if not to love, at least to understand one another."

Edward McCourt, *The Road Across Canada*

As in the days of Sir James Douglas, so now Canada needs the Transcontinental Highway for the unification of her peoples. Had I not seen them — Scotchmen, Irishmen, Welshmen, Old and New Englanders, United Empire Loyalist descendants, picturesque Habitants, the mixed races of the prairies and the mountains, thousands of incoming farmers from the great Republic to the south? Were they not as isolated from each other as if Eastern and Western Canada were worlds remote and unrelated? What might not a connecting road accomplish for such diverse elements as these in common purpose, in common ideals? Does not Canada, as much as India, or Algiers and Tunis, or indeed Europe itself, need that continuous thoroughfare from border to border which has ever stood for unity and strength?

Of course, it takes more than a highway to make a country. But a highway helps, especially one the size of the Trans-Canada, which carries Canadians into all parts of their country to meet the people, feel the immensity and appreciate the landscape. "I know a man whose school could never teach him patriotism," Pierre Trudeau once wrote, "but who acquired that virtue when he felt in his bones the vastness of his land, and the greatness of those who founded it." Trudeau was writing about wilderness canoeing, but the same sentiment holds true for a driving expedition on the Trans-Canada. Ever since its completion, Canadians have been "goin' down the road" to discover what their country is all about. For many of us, the Trans-Canada has replaced the railway as the glue that holds the country together.

Canadians have indulged in a love affair with the open road that is second only to that of our American neighbours. The space beckons. Nine-tenths of us live within a few kilometres of the Trans-Canada, and most of our commerce travels down it. The highway connects the dots of our national existence. It is, in the words of the writer Kildare Dobbs, "the strand on which our scattered communities [are] strung like tiny beads on an infinitely long thread." Dobbs' metaphor

Near the end of his 1912 cross-Canada drive, Thomas Wilby pauses by the shores of Cameron Lake on Vancouver Island, perhaps to ponder the future of highway development in the country.

"There was no better way to see a country and meet its people than to beg for rides along the way, to have long conversations (sometimes very long) with strangers, to test public generosity, to overcome fears, within oneself and in others, and to see the road, and feel it. Standing on a remote rural road, you could see the vastness of what it was attempting to connect. On a suburban on-ramp, you could feel the pulse of a society as it rushed from office to mall to home. And climbing into the cars of that society—at the invitation of a stranger who had everything to lose, as did you—you could sense the openness of the nation, along with its fears and prejudices. In short, you could stand on the roadside and put an entire nation on the couch."

John Stackhouse, *Timbit Nation: A Hitchhiker's View of Canada*

captures the size of the country, along with its contingency. As Canadians know from our periodic constitutional squabbles, the thread might break, the beads might scatter. Meanwhile, the highway reveals us to ourselves.

It serves many other purposes as well. Almost all the products we use in our daily lives are delivered by road. The highway has always been a useful vehicle for political patronage; more than one provincial government has used road-building contracts to reward friends. And it still accounts for a good portion of the tourist dollars that are spent by visitors. But for most of us, the Trans-Canada has a more personal relevance. It is where we spend our holidays, how we visit friends and relatives, the means by which we see our country.

The highway has never become the iconic symbol of national unity that the transcontinental railway once was. This may be in part because of federal-provincial squabbling that marked its funding, planning and construction, and in part because the project dragged on for many

years and its story was more difficult to mythologize than the romantic tale of the CPR. Perhaps it is more useful to think of the Trans-Canada as a metaphor than as a symbol. Like the highway, Canada is in a constant state of becoming. Our country is characterized by an enduring tension between unity and diversity, between the desire to have a common identity that sets us apart and the everyday recognition that we are multiple, fragmented, changeable. The highway reflects both sides of ourselves: it promotes unity by bringing us together, at the same time as it reveals diversity by showing us our complexity. It is truly a road for Canada.

Northwest Passage
By Stan Rogers

Westward from the Davis Strait 'tis there 'twas said to lie
The sea route to the Orient for which so many died;
Seeking gold and glory, leaving weathered, broken bones
And a long-forgotten lonely cairn of stones.

Three centuries thereafter, I take passage overland
In the footsteps of brave Kelso, where his "sea of flowers" began
Watching cities rise before me, then behind me sink again
This tardiest explorer, driving hard across the plain.

And through the night, behind the wheel, the mileage clicking west
I think upon Mackenzie, David Thompson and the rest
Who cracked the mountain ramparts and did show a path for me
To race the roaring Fraser to the sea.

How then am I so different from the first men through this way?
Like them, I left a settled life; I threw it all away
To seek a Northwest Passage at the call of many men
To find there but the road back home again.

CHORUS *Ah, for just one time I would take the Northwest Passage*
To find the hand of Franklin reaching for the Beaufort Sea;
Tracing one warm line through a land so wide and savage
And make a Northwest Passage to the sea.

Acknowledgments

My thanks to Mark Stanton for inviting me to participate in this trip along the Trans-Canada Highway, and to Roberto Dosil for his wonderful design work on the book. Thanks also to Professor Dimitry Anastakis, who reviewed the manuscript, and to Brian Scrivener and Frances Peck, the editors who improved it. Also Tom Cochrane and Darrell Fox for allowing the use of quoted material.

DANIEL FRANCIS
Vancouver, May 4, 2006

SA&D PUBLISHERS would like to thank the following people for their contributions to the project, Arden Phair, Colleen Wood, D. Ariel Rogers, Darrell Fox, Dave Hollins, Dean Kujala, Elizabeth Vincent, Erin McMillan, Lorne Findlay, Rick Hansen, and Sandy Notarianni.

Vancouver, May 25, 2006

This publication would not be possible without the generous support of Don and Barbara Atkins.

Sources

GENERAL

This study of the Trans-Canada Highway is based on a variety of sources, both primary and secondary. They are listed below, under the relevant chapters. More general sources from which I drew information and insights include Norman Ball, ed., *Building Canada: A History of Public Works* (Toronto: University of Toronto Press, 1988); Robert Collins, *A Great Way to Go: The Automobile in Canada* (Toronto: McGraw-Hill Ryerson, 1969); Hugh Durnford and Glenn Baechler, *Cars of Canada* (Toronto: McClelland & Stewart, 1983); James J. Flink, *The Automobile Age* (Cambridge, MA: MIT Press, 1988); J.L. Granatstein, Irving Abella, David J. Bercuson, R. Craig Brown and H. Blair Neatby, eds., *Twentieth Century Canada* (Toronto: McGraw-Hill Ryerson, 1983); Edwin Guillet, *The Story of Canadian Roads* (Toronto: University of Toronto Press, 1966); Desmond Morton, *Wheels: The Car in Canada* (Toronto: Umbrella Press, 1998); Wes Rataushk, *Silver Highway: A Celebration of the Trans-Canada Highway* (Toronto: Fitzhenry & Whiteside, 1988); Jonathan F. Vance, *Building Canada: People and Projects that Shaped the Nation* (Toronto: Penguin Canada, 2006); Bob Weber, *The Longest Road: Stories Along the Trans-Canada Highway* (Red Deer: Red Deer Press, 2003).

PROLOGUE

The description of the official opening ceremony is taken from *The Globe and Mail* for September 4, 1962. W.A.C. Bennett's attitude is described in David Mitchell's biography of the premier, *W.A.C. Bennett and the Rise of British Columbia* (Vancouver: Douglas & McIntyre, 1983). Walter Stewart's comment is from his book *My Cross-Country Checkup* (Toronto: Stoddart, 2000). The calculation about the length of the highway is from Edward J. Marten, "Trans-Canada Highway, 1963," *Canadian Geographical Journal* (September 1963). An interesting discussion of the Canadian Pacific Railway as a symbol of national unity is in Vincent Lavoie, *Primal Images: Transmutations of a National Icon* (Paris: Centre Culturel Canadien, 2004).

CHAPTER ONE

The origins of the highway in British Columbia are described in G.W. Taylor, *The Automobile Saga in British Columbia, 1864–1914* (Victoria: Morriss Publishing, 1984). The adventures of Wilby and Haney are recounted in Thomas Wilby, *A Motor Tour Through Canada* (London: John Lane, 1914) and retold in John Nicol, *The All-Red Route: From Halifax to Victoria in a 1912 Reo* (Toronto: McArthur & Company, 1999). Details of the Gomerys' expedition are in Percy Gomery, *A Motor Scamper 'Cross Canada* (Toronto: Ryerson Press, 1922). Douglas Owram's discussion of car culture is in *Icons and Albatrosses: Passenger Transportation as Policy and Symbol in Canada*, vol. 3 of Report of the Royal Commission on National Passenger Transportation (Ottawa, 1992). The impact of the automobile in the urban environment is the subject of Stephen Davies, "Reckless Walking Must Be Discouraged," *Urban History Review* (October 1989). The best sources for the rise of the motel in North America are Warren James Belasco, *Americans on the Road: From Autocamp to Motel, 1910–45* (Cambridge, MA: MIT Press, 1979) and John A. Jakle, Keith A. Sculle and Jefferson S. Rogers, *The Motel in America* (Baltimore: Johns Hopkins University Press, 1996). The development of other roadside amenities is discussed in John A. Jakle and Keith A. Sculle, *Fast Food: Roadside Restaurants in the Automobile Age* (Baltimore: Johns Hopkins University Press, 1999). An interesting article about the early days of the automobile is Donald Davis's "Dependent Motorization: Canada and the Automobile to the 1930s," *Journal of Canadian Studies* (Fall 1986). The best source for the politics of the highway project is David W. Monaghan, *Canada's "New Main Street": The Trans-Canada Highway as Idea and Reality, 1912–1956* (Ottawa: Canada Science and Technology Museum, 2002).

CHAPTER TWO

The best source for this phase of the project is, again, David Monaghan. The transformation of Canadian society in the 1950s and 1960s is detailed in Douglas Owram, *Born at the Right Time: A History of the Baby-Boom Generation* (Toronto: University of Toronto Press, 1996).

Arthur Lower's book is *Canadians in the Making* (Toronto: Longmans, 1958).

CHAPTER THREE

The construction of the northern Ontario portion of the highway is described in Marcus Van Steen, "The Trans-Canada Highway Makes Road-Building History North of Lake Superior," *Canadian Geographical Journal* (November 1962). The McCourts' adventures are recounted in Edward McCourt, *The Road Across Canada* (Toronto: Macmillan, 1965). The historical context of this period is detailed in J.L. Granatstein, *Canada: 1957–1967* (Toronto: McClelland & Stewart, 1986). The Simon Fraser quotation is from W. Kaye Lamb, ed., *The Letters and Journals of Simon Fraser, 1806–1808* (Toronto: Macmillan, 1960). The completion of the road in Newfoundland is described in Richard Gwyn, *Smallwood: The Unlikely Revolutionary* (Toronto: McClelland & Stewart, 1968) and in vol. 2 of the *Encyclopedia of Newfoundland and Labrador* (St. John's: Newfoundland Book Publishers, 1984). For more on Expo 67 see Pierre Berton, *1967: The Last Good Year* (Toronto: Doubleday, 1997); Robert Fulford, *This Was Expo* (Toronto: McClelland & Stewart, 1968); and Peter C. Newman, *Here Be Dragons: Telling Tales of People, Passion and Power* (Toronto: McClelland & Stewart, 2004). See also Stephen Brook, *Maple Leaf Rag: Travels Across Canada* (London, UK: Hamish Hamilton, 1987).

CHAPTER FOUR

Many roadside attractions encountered along the Trans-Canada are described in Henri Robideau, *Canada's Gigantic!* (Toronto: Summerhill Press, 1988) and in *Canada Coast to Coast,* (Toronto: Reader's Digest, 1998). The Terry Fox story is in Leslie Scrivener, *Terry Fox: His Story* (Toronto: McClelland & Stewart, 1981) and Douglas Coupland, *Terry* (Vancouver: Douglas & McIntyre, 2005). For Rick Hansen, see Rick Hansen and Jim Taylor, *Rick Hansen: Man in Motion* (Vancouver: Douglas & McIntyre, 1987). The section on Prince Edward Island is drawn from Mary K. Cullen, "The Transportation Issue, 1873–1973," in Francis W.P. Bolger, ed., *Canada's Smallest Province: A History of P.E.I.* (Charlottetown: Prince Edward Island

Centennial Commission, 1973). The historical reenactment by John Nicol and Lorne Findlay is the subject of *The All-Red Route*. The Jeffrey Simpson quotation is from his national affairs column in *The Globe and Mail*, September 7, 2005. Pierre Trudeau's reflections on patriotism are in "Exhaustion and Fulfilment: The Ascetic in a Canoe," in Borden Spears, ed., *Wilderness Canada* (Toronto: Clarke, Irwin & Co., 1970). Several travel books have been written about the highway. Aside from the ones already noted, they include Kildare Dobbs, *Ribbon of Highway: By Bus Along the Trans-Canada* (Toronto: Little Brown, 1992); Charles Gordon, *The Canada Trip* (Toronto: McClelland & Stewart, 1997); and John Stackhouse, *Timbit Nation: A Hitchhiker's View of Canada* (Toronto: Random House, 2003).

DANIEL FRANCIS

Index

Credits and Permissions

EVERY REASONABLE EFFORT has been made to trace and contact all holders of copyright and to credit sources correctly. In the event of omission or error SA&D Publishers should be notified so that a full acknowledgment may be made in future editions.

Alain Boily Photo
p.158; 159.
Archives of Ontario
p.33: C301, 575/Newton McConnell fonds; p.63 bottom: C128-5-2-1-20/Duncan Donovan fonds; p.107: top: C7-3, 14294/John Boyd fonds; p.109: RG2-71, VB-42/Audio-Visual Education Branch; p.127: bottom: RG65-35-3, 11764-X2939/Tourism Promotion photographs.
Bibliothèque et Archives Nationales du Québec
p.105: top: E6.S7.SS1.P701609/Gilles Langevin; bottom: E6.S7.SS1.P711064/Henri Rémillard.
Bruce Law Photography
p.14; p.16: top; p.20; 21; p.32: bottom; p.40; 41; 53; 54; 82; 110; 118; 134; 135.
CAA South Central Ontario
p.47; 64.
Canadian Heritage Gallery
© p.18: 23271; p.23: 21934; p.46: 20154; p.68: 20966; p.69: top: 20983; bottom: 20984; p.145: 21035.
Canadian Museum of Civilization
p.140: Catalogue 979.32.8/Image S94-26247; p.141: Catalogue M-180.5/Image S94-26044; Catalogue D6398 a,b/Image S94-25964; Catalogue 980.45.11/Image S94-26004; Catalogue D6424/Image S94-26377; Catalogue 979.121.1/Image S94-26376; Catalogue 978.128.5/Image S94-26253.
Canadian Pacific Railway Archives
p.vi: MNC429/Nicholas Morant; p.116: M7465/Nicholas Morant; p.130: top: A6190/Kenneth
© Shoesmith; bottom: A6189/James Crockart; p.131: A20693.
Canada Post Corporation. Reproduced with permission
p.6: left: POS-000450; right: E001217895; p.58: E001217895; p.174: POS-000502.
Canadian Science and Technology Museum
p.44: 1983.0423.001.S11.AA.CS.
City of Toronto Archives
p.38: Series 0071/Item 7435; p.51: Fonds 1244/Item 1008.
City of Vancouver Archives
p.28: LGN 537/Richard Broadbridge; p.31: bottom: LGN 534/Richard Broadbridge; p.36: CVA 99-3292/Stuart Thompson; p.39: CVA 99-3318/Stuart Thompson; p.99: right: CAN N84.

Coast Imaging Arts
p.60; 61; 147.
CP Images
p.83: 569835; p.86: Jeff McIntosh; p.96: 543143; p.111: Dick Darrell; p.121: Colin Comeau; p.123: Andrew Vaughan; p.151: Boris Spremo; p.164: Mark Taylor; p.167: Don Denton; p.173: Mike DiBattista; p.175: Stephen McGillivray; p.178: Don Denton.
Department of Public Works
p.7: 112.
Ford Motor Company of Canada
p.52: top; p.54; 57.
Glenbow Archives
p.32: top: NA-2336-2; centre: NA-2336-4; p.34: NB-32-33; p.39: top: NC-6-10217; p.45: top: NA-3969-77; bottom: NA-3219-24; p.71: top: NA-5327-741; bottom: NA-5327-748; p.117: left: NA-4868-177.
Gut of Canso Museum and Archives
p.78: AAQ00AA0015.
Jennifer Friesen Photographer
p.163.
Jewish Historical Society of B.C.
p.12: 39077/Leonard Frank; p.15: 90394/Leonard Frank; p.88: 39253/Otto F. Landauer; p.108: 38442/Otto F. Landauer.
John Sylvester Photography
p.iv; 10; 48; 66; 76; 90; 100; 125; 128; 142; 148; 150; 157; 162; 166; 168.
Ken Steacy Collection
p.84; 85; 144.
Library and Archives Canada
p.2: E006580623; p.3: E006580621; p.29: PA-0229916; p.6: left: POS-000450; right: E001217895; p.31: top: PA-0229919; p.43: PA-040671; p.52: left: PA-053708; p.58: E001217895; p.72: PA-041162; p.73: NMC-7051; p.74: PA-196291; p.79: PA-152321; p.80: E000760672; p.99: left: C-000211; centre: PA-196291; p.102: left: PA-191984; p.107: PA-111479; p.117: PA-111479; p.120: A210462K; p.122: PA-211487; p.127: top: A206917K; p.136: E004665424; p.137: left: E000990867; right: E000990971; p.139: E001098961; p.146: E003719025; p.174: POS-000502; p.177: PA-029917.
The Montreal Museum of Fine Arts
p.161: 1914.94/George B. Cramp Bequest. Photo: Christine Guest.
Musée de la civilisation
p.92: 1998-385/Donation Michel Masse. Photo: Idra Labrie.
Musée Du Bas-Saint-Laurent
p.50: 102979/Fonds Ulric Lavoie.
McCord Museum of Canadian History, Montreal
p.70: M965.199.5962/*Another Trans-Canada Highway Problem*; p.97: M965.199.5990/*Our New National Anthem*.

Natural Resources Canada
p.81 and 171: 1981-MCR4050; p.102: 1955-085; p.172: 1983-MCR4120.
Newfoundland & Labrador Provincial Archives
p.133: B-8-78.
Pacific Newspaper Group Inc.
p.154: John Vanyshyn; p.155: Ian Lindsay; p.156: Les Bazso.
Rob D'Estrube Photographer
p.84; p.85: top left.
Roberto Dosil
p.35; 37; 42; 56; 59; 95; 114; 115; 119.
British Columbia Archives
p.17: I-68231; p.20: EDH186B; p.21: EDH186C; p.22: I-68233; p.23: I-68234; p.24: NWP388.1 W666C; p.26: I-68235; p.30: top: EDH186-IC; centre: EDH186-IA; bottom: EDH186-IB.
Saskatchewan Archives Board
p.104: R-B4711-8.
St. Catharines Museum
p.16: top: Donation Michael Guzei; p.16: bottom: 004657; p.25: Donation Lowell A. Haney.
The Globe and Mail PhotoStore
p.89: 3.010404.
Travis Favretto Photography
p.5; 106; 124; 165; 176.
Vancouver Public Library, Special Collections
p.62: 33688; p.98: 34138; p.112: 33962; p.132: 33870.
Whyte Museum of the Canadian Rockies
p.113: V263NA-71-1707; p.170: V469-1558.

The following individuals and organizations generously contributed material from their archives and collections.

Ariel Rogers, Fogarty's Cove Music
p.179.
A&W Food Services of Canada Inc.
p.61.
Darrell Fox, Terry Fox Foundation
p.153.
Dave Hollins
p.53; 54; 56; 59; 61; 62; 82; 95; 114; 115; 119; 134; 135.
Janice Ryan
p.19.
Lorne Findlay
p.16: top; 19; 35.
Perkins Bull Foundation and Black Creek Pioneer Village, Toronto and Region Conservation Authority
p.160.
Quita Francis
p.110.

Stanton Atkins & Dosil Publishers
Mailing address
2632 Bronte Drive
North Vancouver, BC
Canada V7H 1M4

National Library of Canada Cataloguing in Publication

Francis, Daniel,
      A Road for Canada: The Illustrated Story of the
      Trans-Canada Highway
Includes bibliographical references and index
ISBN 0-9732346-7-9

Edited by: Brian Scrivener
Designed by: Roberto Dosil
Map by: Angela Atkins, Dean Kujala
Printed by: C&C Offset Printing
Co., Ltd.(China)

This book's titles, text,
sidebars and captions are
set in Scala Regular and
Scala Sans, a typeface family
designed by Martin Majoor
between 1990 and 1998.